Future Church

by David Cox

Editor: David Marshall BA PhD

Acknowledgements and thanks to: Nan Tucker,
Professor John Walton and Andrew Hardy BA MTh,
who read and critiqued the manuscript.

David Cox is also the author of
Think Big Think Small Groups
published by the Department of Personal Ministries
at the South England Conference of
Seventh-day Adventists.

Future Church
Copyright © 2001 David Cox

All rights reserved. No part of this publication may be reproduced
in any form without prior permission from the publisher.

British Library Cataloguing in Publication Data.
A catalogue record for this book is available
from the British Library.

ISBN 1-899505-77-6

First published 2001

Printed and Published by
The Stanborough Press Ltd,
Alma Park, Grantham,
Lincs., England, NG31 9SL.

Acknowledgements

It's hard to know where to begin and where to end. I am blessed by so many people who inspire, encourage and challenge me that it would probably be the simplest thing to say 'Thank God for His church', of which they are all a part. In almost every congregation I have visited over the past year or two, I have talked with forward-thinking believers, young and old, who love the church and want to see it grow and, where necessary, change, to become more than it is at the moment. To these visionary disciples of Jesus I am thankful. But I need to be a bit more specific than that.

Firstly, I acknowledge my wife, Velda, once again as my best critic, and thank her for the endless hours she has given sharing ideas, making suggestions, and discussing the manuscript as it has developed. After her, our two sons, Andrew and Bryan, have helped me see the church and what it needs to be through more youthful eyes.

Don MacFarlane, president of the South England Conference, continues to inspire me by his openness to change and his willingness for churches and leaders to try new things. Aris Vontzalides and Humphrey Walters continue to serve as my personal mentors: as we have met frequently to discuss and pray for the future of the church, they have been a source of great support for this book project. I also greatly value the visionary ministry of Peter Roennfeldt, Ministerial secretary for the Trans European Division.

And how can I fail to mention the members of my small group – Ashwin, Gita, Beverley, Mac, Steve, Tone, Jeanette and Karin – along with Trevor and Rene Clarke's group in Brixton, Jeremy, Sheila and Shirley's group in Winnersh and Aris's group in Northolt, who demonstrate in their relationships with each other, and their concern for their friends, what authentic Christian community could be like for all of us?

The line drawings you see on many pages of this book, which say so much more than words, are the work of Laurent Grisel. For the changes you don't see which were made to the text before it was published, which make it more comprehensible and less open to misunderstanding, I am indebted to my publishers.

Having said all that, however, I come back to the original Source of all inspiration and all knowledge, Jesus Christ Himself, the living Lord of the Church, and the One who loved the Church so much that He gave Himself for it, so that it might one day become all that He ever knew it could be. Thanks be to God.

Dream Church

This is the Church of my dreams –
The Church of the warm heart,
Of the open mind,
Of the adventurous spirit;
The Church that cares,
That heals hurt lives,
That comforts old people,
That challenges youth;
That knows no divisions of culture or class;
No frontiers, geographical or social;
The Church that enquires as well as affirms,
That looks forward as well as backward:
The Church of the Master,
The Church of the people;
High as the ideals of Jesus,
Low as the humblest human;
A working Church,
A worshipping Church,
A winsome Church;
A Church that interprets truth in terms of truth;
That inspires courage for this life
and hope for the life to come;
A Church of courage;
The Church of all good men –
The Church of the living God.

Anon

All Bible quotations are taken from the Good News Bible
unless otherwise stated.

The Question Is

'Does YOUR church have a future?'

'Today's church is incapable of responding to the present moral crisis. It must reinvent itself, or face virtual oblivion by mid-21st century.'[1]

Isn't the church an extraordinary, marvellous thing! Made up of ordinary people like you and me, it is very, very human. But, as the body of Christ, it is wonderfully divine. So what can be said about this divine-human miracle except that it will always fall short of what it could be, and that it can always become more than it is? That is also true of this book. Because it is about the church, it falls far short of what it could be and, in a year or so, could be rewritten in a far better way. But I trust that its shortcomings will not obscure its central challenge: that we face the future with all its possibilities honestly, optimistically, and with an open mind. And that we dare to begin by addressing the question, *'Does YOUR church have a future?'*

Not so long ago it would have been unheard of to ask such a question. The Second Advent movement of which we are a part was raised up by God for a special time with a special message, and so we could confidently state on our baptism and church membership certificate, *'I believe that the Seventh-day Adventist Church is the remnant church of Bible prophecy into which people of every nation, race, and language are invited and accepted. And I desire membership in its fellowship.*[2]

I joined the church at a time when the truth was the truth and there was only one way to live it. People were either 'in the truth' or they were out of it. Adventists were Adventists: you knew one when you saw one. Adventist churches were Adventist churches: services in one were like services in another, and we all sang from the same hymnbook (in Britain it was the *New Advent Hymnal*, and it was still new thirty years after it was published). Evangelists were still doing – successfully – what they had always done, the church was growing and, just as Christ had promised, *'the gates of hell [would] not prevail against it.'*[3]

A few decades later, it's a different picture. Take an honest look around and it's obvious that the gates of hell have definitely prevailed against some churches. Thousands of church buildings up and down the country still serve their communities, not as centres of worship but as bingo halls, garages, clubs, and even Muslim mosques and Sikh temples. Many once-strong congregations are now in decline; the members are elderly; and, unless there's a change for the better,  still more church buildings will become 'available'. Other congregations are bravely struggling for survival, and many of them are Seventh-day Adventist.

Many congregations are growing, of course, but even that good news raises other causes for concern. As with other Christian denominations, it seems as though the face of some Adventist churches is changing. We no longer all use the same music, and some congregations have changed the way they 'do church'. In some places the study of the Sabbath school lesson is no longer a requirement, and even our theology and lifestyle seem to differ from place to place. We're more conservative in some places, more liberal in others, and the differences between the two 'sides' are so great we are not too sure what to make of it. Some say the changes are for the better; others say the church is becoming 'more worldly'. Going the contemporary route is seen by some as the only way to go. Others see it as playing into the devil's hands.

Wherever you are in all of this, no doubt you share a number of common concerns about the present situation. While you are most likely optimistic about the future, because you know it's in God's hands, you probably wonder how we should respond to the enormous challenges it presents us with. It's no secret:

- While the church is growing rapidly in some areas of the world, it is declining in others.
- Evangelistic methods that served us well for many years no longer produce the same results.
- Even where our evangelistic strategy is reasonably successful, the large majority of our converts come from a very small segment of the population. In Northern Europe, for instance, Adventists have little or no real impact among secular, unchurched people who make up 80-90% of the population. Similarly, the large minority groups, such as Asians and Chinese, Jews and Muslims living in some of our cities, have not responded to our traditional evangelistic methods at all.
- Some other churches seem to be succeeding where we are failing to reach unchurched people.
- Many converts leave the church within a few years of joining, especially if they joined as the result of a public

evangelistic campaign. Worse still, too many young people who have grown up in the church have left by the time they are eighteen.

- It seems that most of those who leave the church do so not because they don't believe the doctrines any more. The reasons they give include the following, and we need to hear what they say:
  - failure to experience God in their lives as promised from the pulpit;
  - lack of support in times of personal discouragement and spiritual crisis with the organization;
  - sense of personal failure to live according to the requirements of the church;
  - negative experiences with fellow church members or leaders, e.g. gossip, judgemental attitudes;
  - irrelevance of church to everyday life;
  - marriage to a non-Adventist partner;
  - moving to a new city or country where the new church is slow to accept them;
  - general disillusionment with the organization.

Such facts cause me concern. As we see evidences of a renewed interest in spiritual things around us,[4] we can't just blame 'the world' or a 'lack of commitment' for these problems. Neither can we say that people are just too busy these days, because people usually find time to do what they really want to do. I have to face the uncomfortable possibility that I may be part of the problem, and that as a church we could be partly or largely responsible for the difficulties we now face.

Changing times

As already observed, the times they are a-changin'. That's

nothing new of course: this church of ours was born in a time of economic, social and religious upheaval. But change today is taking place much faster than ever before, and it's happening in every area of life. Neither is it simply external, superficial change we are seeing, as in the workplace, the fashion and music industries, and the market place. We're talking about *serious* change, fundamental changes in attitudes, in the way people think about themselves and the world they live in, and how they express themselves.[5] Even more to the point, such change has altered the way people experience or perceive the church. For that reason alone, my future church *must* come to terms with what is called the 'post-modern culture' and prayerfully search for ways of relating with it effectively.

In a recent lecture presented to an international audience of church leaders,[6] church-growth consultant Carl George observed that *'the post-modern phase of our culture already tears at our most cherished assumptions. It is pushing us out of our comfort zone, how we preach, minister and evangelize. Our world is said to be moving from the industrial age to the information age, dominated by machines called electronic, intelligent, digital and interactive.'* He then listed a number of characteristics of today's Western world which help define the challenge we face as Christians, and suggested how the church might adapt its methods accordingly. Here are some of them:

- **Interactive**. Post-modern people are not prepared to sit and listen to a long lecture or sermon for fifty minutes: they want to be involved. The best way growing churches can meet this challenge is through small-group ministry, and by making worship services and other public meetings as interactive and participatory as possible.

- **Mobility**. This is the age of multiple choice, whether in terms of television channels, breakfast cereals, employment – or churches. For example, many people tend to move from one employer to another  as they develop professionally, instead of staying with the same employer for life as folk once did. In the same way, there is the growing trend of people attending the church that best meets their needs at a paticular period in their lives (e.g. parents with small children will often travel considerable distances to attend a church which has a good children's Sabbath school programme. When the children are older they find their own church to attend and the parents settle for a church closer to home.) We may not endorse this trend ourselves, but one way we can respond to this reality is to accept that we need different churches for different people.

- **Music Experience**. Music today is experienced more than it is listened to. People are interested in music that does something to them. In church they do not care to sing just from a sense of duty but because they are inspired and moved by the music. The music speaks not only to their minds but also to their souls. This particular challenge is met in the choice of music, in the way it is led and the context in which it happens.

- **Suspicion of Authority**. People no longer automatically trust authority figures, either in society or in the church. The public no longer holds teachers, doctors, and the police in high regard. At one time vicars, priests and pastors were highly respected in society for the position they held, but not any more. Today they are respected and trusted not for their position in society but for who they are individually, for what they have to offer, for their interest in people and the time they give to people.

* **Authenticity**. One reason for the suspicion mentioned above is that individuals and institutions turned out to be 'phoney' – different from what they claimed to be. Today's Christians must be genuine. We simply have to be who we claim to be, and not claim to be more than we are. As the song says, Christians must 'walk the walk' as well as 'talk the talk'. That means being honest about our failures as well as our successes. The Good News is that Jesus makes a difference in the bad times as well as the good.

* **Equality of the Sexes**. Post-modern people are consciously discarding the discriminations of the cultural or religious past, especially this one. Sexual equality is not just a matter of political correctness: it is part and parcel of modern thinking and practice. The church must therefore be extremely careful, sensitive and persuasive, if it chooses to treat men and women differently in any significant way. If we teach that in Christ there is no Jew or Gentile, bond or free, male or female, we must be seen to operate consistently by that principle.

* **Intolerant of Coercion**. New millennium people see traditional religion as built upon coercion, and do not respond to appeals to duty. On the other hand, they are very responsive to people who will take time to hang out with them and use persuasion, instead of shaming efforts to manipulate or coerce their behaviour.

- **Close-to-the-Edge Living**. Modern people admire those who take risks, whether in the way they dress or their choice of sports. We should not be shocked if visitors turn up at church in unconventional attire, or if young people who have grown up in the church appear to be 'rebellious' in the way they dress or use jewellery. It would be a mistake to interpret such things according to the values of a previous generation.

- **Excellence**. Mediocrity may have been good enough in yesterday's world, but it isn't good enough now. Churches and Christians should offer only their best in worship and service.

- **Story-telling**. New millennium people respond more readily to stories of what Jesus has done in the life of a person than to some logical and impressive presentation on some aspect of religion. In this respect they communicate as people did in bygone ages. Jesus used a lot of stories in communicating the Gospel. So a leading question today is no longer 'Is Christianity true?' but 'Does Christianity work?'

The Issue of 'The Truth'. Here's a sensitive and delicate subject, and I risk being misunderstood by raising it, but it's important to our ability to communicate the Gospel in these changing times, so I'll raise it anyway. The search for truth always has been, and always must be, central to the progress of Adventism. But what is truth? Pilate's question is still being asked, probably by more people than ever before, and it's our task to answer it. In trying to answer it, however, we need to remember that although 'the truth' hasn't changed and never will, the way contemporary people in the Western world think about truth has.

Obviously God Himself is the ultimate or absolute Truth, so His Word and all that flows from Him is ultimately and absolutely true for all time and for all people. As the prophet points out, it is because of the way God is, and because the way He works never changes, that we can have a solid hope of eternal life. (Mal. 3:6.) Likewise, Jesus is *'the same, yesterday, today and forever.'*[7] Does everyone see this truth? Can it be communicated in terms acceptable to the 21st century?

Jesus Himself taught that although the law is eternal and unchangeable[8] (because of its association with the eternal and unchangeable Law-Giver) it has meaning only when understood in terms of meaningful relationships. He insisted that *'the whole law of Moses and the teachings of the prophets* [i.e. 'the truth'] *depend on these two commandments'*[9] of love for God and love for people. While the letter of the law is true, it has little value if the spirit of the law is absent. It was an idea which seriously upset the religious leaders of His day, but it should not unsettle us. After all, truth is only relevant for me if I can see and understand how it affects my life and my connections with the world I live in and the people I live among. This has always been the case, of course, but modern people are probably less easily satisfied with form and more concerned with substance than previous generations.

Take the subject of the Sabbath, for example. In days gone by all we had to do was to prove that the Sabbath was on Saturday, not Sunday, and an honest person would accept it. But not any more. Post-modern people have to go beyond the claim that the Sabbath is 'true' to something more personal, namely, 'What difference will it make in my life?' It's a fair question. The Sabbath has only ever had significance because of the part it was designed to play in man's relationships with God and his fellow man. It's just that we are more aware of the real issues these days, and our message will only have maximum impact when we can direct it not only to people's minds but also to their hearts. We will look at this in more detail in chapter five.

A Different Planet? If you find all this just a bit unsettling, you are in good company. Today's youth and young adults really do live in a different world from that of their

parents. It's not just the 'generation gap' syndrome which has always separated generations from one another: it's the post-modern world we are living in, and, for all practical purposes, it's like living on a different planet.

And perhaps that's not such a bad thing anyway. After all, are we not heading for a home and a lifestyle that really is 'out of this world'? As Christians – as a church – we should never get to the place where we are satisfied with who we are, what we believe, or what we have achieved. Thankful, yes, but not satisfied. Until Christ's return, we must always be moving forward to what we can become, rather than backward to what we once were. We may need revival and reformation, but only as spurs towards ongoing growth and maturity. Change in God's order of things means giving up nothing of value, only those things which hinder progress. According to Leith Anderson, the role of spiritual leaders is to see to it that this kind of growth continues:

'Leaders must keep calling the organisation and its people back to the Lordship of Jesus Christ and the standards of the

Bible while challenging people to grow and innovate within the Biblical boundaries. Fulfilling the mission is always more important than perpetuating traditions.'[10]

True to our roots. Once upon a time, the church, like Jesus, was God's agent for revolutionary change in a more or less static society. The Seventh-day Adventist Church began in the same way, which is why the pioneers saw themselves as a movement, rather than just another church. Sadly, the Christian Church in general is now conservative by nature and resistant to change in a world that is hardly the same from one day to the next. Is the Adventist Church any different? It must be. Maybe we have become something of an institution and less like the dynamic movement we started out as, but these are times of unparalleled challenge and unequalled opportunity. The new millennium calls for a renewed church. And that means a church that is willing to go the way of the cross – the way of self-sacrifice. It's the way of the pioneers.

It occurs to me that what Jesus once said about the survival of individual Christians also applies to churches, namely that *'a grain of wheat remains no more than a single grain unless it is dropped into the ground and dies,'*[11] and that *'if you try to save your life, you will lose it. But if you give it up for me, you will surely find it.'*[12] Do you get the point? The church which is interested only in self-preservation isn't going anywhere. But the church which gives everything, even itself, for the needs of others, will survive and grow.

There's no question about the survival of *the* church. Jesus gave up His own life, and like a grain of wheat was cast into the ground and died. Because of that great sacrifice alone, there will be a great harvest. There will also be a harvest because countless Christians and countless congregations through the ages have followed His example. So, yes, the church has a future. But that's not the issue. The issue is,' Does *your* church have a future?'

Honestly, now, are you satisfied with your present church? Or are you one of an increasing number of Adventists who sense that although they belong to a wonderful, world-wide family, they still have some growing to do? Do you believe that maintaining the status quo will see us through successfully to the second coming of Jesus, or do you share the conviction that it's time for change? Not wholesale change, of course, because some things are changeless. Who can change the everlasting Gospel? No, I'm talking simply about changes that *your* church may choose to make as a result of the Spirit's leading you from where you are now to where He wants you to be in the future.

I for one believe there is a need for such change. But I don't offer this book as a catalogue of changes which your church should make. I simply want to address certain areas of church life which we need to look at from time to time and ask seriously and prayerfully:

- Is my church communicating effectively with the world of the 21st century?
- How well do we compare with the New Testament model of the church?
- Are we working, witnessing, worshipping and growing together in harmony with the inspired guidelines? Or do we need to change direction in order to be faithful to what God has already told us?
- Do we need to keep doing all that we are doing? If so, could we do it better than we are doing it now?
- Are we the best stewards we can be of the resources God has given us to invest in and care for?
- Is it possible God is trying to say something to us, but

we're not listening because we're too busy doing what we've always done?

Over the past few years, like many others, I have tried to address questions like these as honestly as I could, and it's been an uphill struggle. The proverbial 'baggage', both personal and institutional, has weighed me down. But trying to do better is like climbing a mountain – it's tough, but exhilarating. And I've seen and experienced enough in my church to be able to say that although we have some way to go I'm excited about climbing the next peak, and I'm optimistic that we'll get there.

Hence this book. It's all about being the church God wants us to be, doing what He wants us to do, and doing it the way He wants it done. Its about becoming an authentic Christian community, fulfilling the dream of Christ that we may be one just as He and the Father are one.[13] It's about growth, and that means it's about evangelism, although there's not a particular chapter about that. Evangelism, after all, is not an event or a programme, but part of a way of life. Churches are living things, and living things grow naturally, if they are healthy. So the emphasis here is not so much on 'soul-winning' but on building healthy churches that grow.[14]

Does your church have a future, then? I should like to think so. But the bottom line – the inescapable fact – is that the future of your church is up to you and the rest of your church family. Your church will survive and thrive only if it's healthy. Thankfully, there is no doubt about the future of

God's Church, whatever the Sunday newspapers say. His work on Earth is going to end in a greater blaze of glory than that which marked its opening, and all the signs are that the stage is being set for that to happen. And your future church can be there to see the finale.

---

[1] George Barna, *The Second Coming of the Church* (Nashville, Tennessee, U.S.A.: Word Publishing, 1998), front cover.

[2] Statement 13 on the British certificate of Membership/Baptism until it was replaced recently by a new certificate which carries no doctrinal statements of belief.

[3] Matthew 16:18.

[4] e.g. The development of house churches and the many new congregations that have grown out of them during the past thirty years, and the spread of New Age philosophy, especially among young adults in Western society.

[5] Youth culture, feminism, trade in illegal drugs, sexual liberation, globalization, environmental pollution, the peace movement following two world wars, Vietnam, and the development of nuclear power, to name a few examples, have all had a profound effect on how people live their lives and view past, present and future. In his fascinating book, *Sacred Cows Make Gourmet Burgers*, William Easum suggests that the fundamental shift from a Newtonian view of science which has dominated our thinking for the past few hundred years, to Einstein's quantum theories which now determine how we interpret life's experiences, is one of the primary reasons for many of the changes we have seen in recent years. (Nashville, U.S.A.: Abingdon Press, 1995) chapter 2.

[6] 'New Culture – New Church' Conference, San Antonio, Texas, September 1999. We may not agree with him on everything, but we do need to be aware that he is describing the way people 'out there' are thinking.

[7] Hebrews 13:8.

[8] Matthew 5:17, 18.

[9] Matthew 22:40.

[10] Leith Anderson, *Dying for Change* (Minneapolis, U.S.A.: Bethany House, 1998), page 136.

[11] John 12:24.

[12] Matthew 10:39 (Contemporary English Version).

[13] John 17:20-23.

[14] An excellent 'health-check' questionnaire for local churches is the one developed by Christian A. Schwartz in connection with his book *Natural Church Development* (Moggerhanger, Beds, UK: British Church Growth Association, 1996). Copies are available from the Personal Ministries Department of the South England Conference.

Chapter One

The Love Affair
A parable

'The angel also showed me the river of the water of life, sparkling like crystal, and coming from the throne of God and of the Lamb and flowing down the middle of the city's street. . . . The Spirit and the Bride say, "Come!" Everyone who hears this must also say, "Come!" Come, whoever is thirsty; accept the water of life as a gift, whoever wants it.'[1]

The kingdom of heaven is like a river.[2] From high up in the mountains it came, coursing down over rocks and stones and between wooded slopes until it reached the plain. There it flowed, wide and strong, reflecting the glory of the sun above, giving life to the

city that had grown up beside it. It satisfied the city's thirst, watered its crops, and provided fish for food. Young people and children played in its shallows. There was prosperity and health for all.

Gradually the city grew and developed. The people built docks and parks and bridges, and added sluices and water-wheels to harness the river's force. One idea led to another, and eventually the idea of a dam came up. How much more could be achieved by a great dam, which would store the river's mighty power and give constant energy that didn't vary with the seasons.

And so a dam was built, bringing new benefits to the city – at first. But little by little, the dam brought changes. As time passed, there was less and less of a river and more and more of a lake. Not only that, but the water didn't seem to sparkle any more. In fact, sometimes sickness and disease came to the city, but the changes in the water happened so gradually that no one connected them with the problems they now began to experience.

Meanwhile, something else was happening. The pure water kept flowing down from the mountains, and with time the level of the water gradually rose behind the dam. Then one spring as the snows began to melt on the mountains, the river started swelling to new levels. Early one April morning the people woke up to a sound they had never heard before – the sound of rushing, roaring water, and they ran to the river to see what was happening. The dam was still there – but the water was rapidly flowing away. The dam itself had not broken, but the earth wall to the side of it had given way, and a foaming cascade of water was thundering through the breach. The water level began to go down, and the mud and filth of many years were swept away as the river poured forth in new power.

Confusion filled the city. Who was responsible for this disaster? Was it sabotage? Was it the work of terrorists? Experts met to discuss the situation, and went on television to say that there was nothing to worry about – everything was under control. But not everyone believed them. Engineers inspected the damage and made their reports, but there was little they could do. The river had cut a new course for itself as it surged across the plain, and no one was able to close the breach or stop the flow. Officials did the only sensible thing they could think of – they put up 'Danger, keep out!' signs near the new river, and the city council passed a series of resolutions forbidding anyone to go near it. All that remained of the old river was a dirty, stagnant, stream flowing sluggishly along the river bed, only a shadow of its former self.

Time passed, however, and the city learned to live with the situation, as cities do. Most people contented themselves with living their lives, taking care of the dam (now nearly useless) and writing books to explain what had happened. Life returned almost to normal. But a small group of people thought otherwise. They said, 'What's the point of staying here by a useless dam and a sluggish river? Let's move further down the valley and build a new city by the new river.' And so they did.

The city council did not approve. They accused the group of civil disobedience and threatened them with gaol, but these people knew what they wanted and no one was going to stop them getting it. So they set out from the old city and built a new city a few miles away. With time the new city grew and prospered, drawing its life from the powerful flow of the river and its clean fresh water. Docks and parks and bridges were built. The people found ways to harness the river's force, and built sluices and waterwheels and such. There was prosperity and health for all. Until one day, a hundred years or so after the city was founded, someone said, 'I've got a great idea. Let's make a dam. . . .'

And we know the rest of the story, first because history has a way of repeating itself, and second because we're all a part of it. It's the story of the love affair – the great romance which God began with us when He created the world, made us in His image, and invited us to live in His presence and draw our life from His life. It's the story of how it almost ended in disaster because of sin; how Satan with his lies made our first parents afraid of God and caused them to run away and hide from Him. And it's the story of how the love affair has been given a second chance because Jesus came to this world to live, suffer and die for us, to affirm His love and win us back; to say that in spite of all we have done and failed to do God's love for us is still the same.

Despite the dam which sin had built, God's love kept flowing from above; the level kept rising; the pressure kept increasing, until it could not be held back any longer, and it burst upon the world in an irre-  sistible tide that nothing could stop. 'For God loved the world so much that he gave his only Son, so that everyone who believes in him may not die but have eternal life.'[3] Once again there's a fountain flowing, deep and wide. And all of us can live again, because of that fountain. Just as the river from the mountains was the source of life to the city, so the love of God is the source of our lives, and without it we're just existing.

There's only one problem. What the adversary did in the beginning he is still doing. The effect of sin now is the same as the effect of sin then. While love and life go side by side – for God is love – and we can no more truly live without love than breathe without air, there is a mysterious resistance to it in our hearts. We don't want God – or anyone else for that matter – to get too close. It's almost as if we have lost the ability to receive and give love the way we were intended to in the beginning.

By nature we are afraid of God, afraid of His Spirit. So we

try to run away and hide from Him. We resist His love; we limit it by our definitions of it; we build our dams to contain it and control it, and we substitute it with other things. The river of love no longer flows as it once did, and life loses its sparkle. It happens to people, and it happens to churches:

- Max decides to follow Jesus for the first time, and his life takes on a new richness and sweetness. Until he starts looking in the mirror, as most new Christians do, and begins to wonder how he can possibly make it to heaven. He becomes preoccupied with the rules and loses sight of the Person, and being a Christian becomes hard work.

- Newtown church starts as a warm, loving fellowship of Christians and their friends who really want to make a difference in their community. Yet within a few years it is hardly recognizable. Services have become routine; people attend from a sense of duty; members are critical and judgemental; and they're more concerned about the music the young people listen to and the clothes they wear than the fact that they come to church. It talks about 'reaching the lost', but it has lost touch with the real world where 'the lost' actually live.

Tragic, isn't it? Because only one thing gives life, only one thing changes us and makes us grow; only one thing saves – and that is the love of God in Christ, communicated to us like a river of living water by the Holy Spirit. It's true for individual Christians, and it's true for churches.

So the question we must answer individually and together is, where are *we* living, and what water are *we* drinking? Is our church more like the old city or the new? Is the water we drink and offer to others stale, or fresh and sparkling? *'"Whoever believes in me, streams of life-giving water will pour out from his heart."' Jesus said this about the Spirit, which those who believed in Him were going to receive.'* (see John 7:37-39.) As we observed before, the parable of the river is the story of life – the story of the relationship between God and the human family from the beginning to the present day. It's been told in many other ways of course, including the version Adventists are most familiar with – *The Great Controversy* or *The Conflict of the Ages.* At the heart of the conflict is the church, *'the only object on earth upon which Christ bestows His supreme regard,'*[4] and therefore also the focus of the adversary's destructive influence. The church is the city in the parable. It is the steward of heaven's blessings, the channel of God's grace, and the bearer of the invitation to *'"Come, whoever is thirsty; accept the water of life as a gift, whoever wants it."'*[5] But 'the church', at least in Scriptural terms, is people, just as cities are, and each member or citizen shares the responsibility for the health of the community. So the parable has something to say to individual church members too. It's about you, and it's about me.

Both new Christians and new churches usually begin well, but it's so easy to lose the plot and forget why we're here. Even the New Testament church, empowered by the Spirit of Pentecost and driven by the passion of Christ to seek and to save lost people, within a few short years was missing the point. It was still doctrinally pure; evangelism was still high on the agenda; and it was still growing numerically, even in the face of persecution. But all of these things counted for nothing, and it risked losing its place in the kingdom of God, because, as the Lord of the church explained, *'you don't have as much love as you used to.'*[6] Interestingly, Christ's warning of rejection to His servants in the final chapter of the drama carries a similar rebuke.[7] They are *'lukewarm, neither hot nor cold'* and need to purchase gold, white clothes and medicine for their eyes, which we understand to represent love and trust, and a saving, life-changing connection with Christ and the Holy Spirit.[8]

Apparently, the underlying problem is the same with both first and last churches. It's a problem of the heart. We may know *about* God, yet not know Him personally. We may be well acquainted with the Bible, but be a stranger to its Author. Christians may belong to a church, but understand nothing of one another's hopes and fears. They may be very active in 'witnessing', but have no interest in the individual needs of those they want to win. There is plenty of activity, but not much passion. So principles and programmes become more important than people. 'Doing church' as we've always done it becomes more important than meeting people where they are. The letter of the law takes over from the spirit of the law. Lifestyle issues and the church's own reputation become more important than grace and the reputation of the Father, who simply wants His children home. The church scores high on developing organization but low on creating community. It's busy and concerned with many things – but what about its love? What about *our* love? Our love for God? Our love for one another? Our love for people?

The fact is that without love nothing we do is worth anything.[9] Intentionally increasing membership without intentionally encouraging the development of deep, caring friendships between believers is pointless, because the church is first of all the body of Christ, in which every part or member is connected with every other.[10] Doctrine, church standards and lifestyle issues, important as they are, have no meaning outside of loving relationships with God and with one another.[11] According to Jesus, what convinces unbelievers about Christianity is not overwhelming argument, nor a well-prepared or well-presented Bible study or sermon, but a community of Christians who love one another.[12] The 'truth' which God and angels long to share with the human family, which sets us free, and which lies at the heart of what Christians have to say to the world before Christ returns, is not a set of rules, nor a list of beliefs, nor a lifestyle, but the person of Jesus.[13]

The church, then, is not first of all a building or an organization, but a group of people who are connected by the love of God to one another and to Christ, and genuinely care about other people too (although if buildings and organization help to keep the family together, fine). So we have to come back to the question, where are we? Which city do we live in? Is the water we are drinking life-giving water or stagnant? Do we simply believe the message, or do we love the Person? Could you describe your relationship and your church's relationship with Jesus right now as a love affair?

It's a fair question. It's what church is all about. And just as friends or married couples occasionally need to evaluate their relationship and make whatever changes are necessary to ensure ongoing growth and maturity, so Christians and churches need to take stock of their position, assess their performance, and be sure they are on course towards where they believe God wants them to be in the future. And that's the burden of this book – that your future church will be the kind of church a lost world nearing its end so desperately needs it to be, one that is in touch with God and in touch with people.

There was a church like this once before, and it had such an impact on society that observers said it *"turned the world upside down."*[14] According to inspiration, there will be such a church once again, except that it will be much bigger and more wonderful, embracing men, women and children from *"every race, tribe, language, and nation."*[15] Its presence will bathe the entire world in light[16] and its impact will be that of a universal Pentecost.

You can help your present church become that future church. And you can begin by doing a bit of prayerful dreaming.

---

[1] Revelation 22:1, 2, 17.

[2] Adapted from the original form I came across some time ago in a book whose title I have since forgotten. Apologies to the author.

[3] John 3:16.

[4] Ellen G. White, *Testimonies to Ministers*, page 49.

[5] Revelation 22:17.

[6] Revelation 2:4 (The Contemporary English Version).

[7] The rebuke of Christ to the church at Ephesus quoted above, Ellen White applies to the remnant church of the last days. She also applies His rebuke to the Pharisees (Matthew 23:2-7, 23) to those who have lost from the heart their 'first love' and describes in contrast a trusting, loving relationship with Him as drinking from the fountain of the water of life. See *Selected Messages*, vol. 1, pages 387, 388.

[8] Revelation 3:16 (ibid). See also comment on verse 18 in SDA *Bible Commentary* (ibid: 1980) vol. 7, 762.

[9] If in doubt, read 1 Corinthians 13.

[10] 1 Corinthians 12, particularly verse 27.

[11] "'Love the Lord your God with all your heart, with all your soul, and with all your mind.' This is the greatest and the most important commandment. The second most important commandment is like it: 'Love your neighbour as you love yourself.' The whole law of Moses and the teachings of the prophets depend on these two commandments."' (Matthew 22:37-40.)

[12] John 13:35.

[13] John 8:32, 36.

[14] Acts 17:6, NKJV.

[15] Revelation 14:6.

[16] Revelation 18:1.

Chapter Two

Dreams and Visions

Seeing tomorrow's church today

'The one thing that is worse than blindness is to have no vision.' – Helen Keller.

Dreams – especially inspired dreams – have tremendous power to change things, not least because such dreams have a way of coming true. Top athletes break records not just because they are fitter or stronger than others but because they are highly motivated by the vision – the mental picture – of running faster or jumping higher than anyone before them. High achievers and successful people in all walks of life are not necessarily the most clever or the most privileged. But they are the most ambitious, and ambitions are born of dreams.

The Bible has power to change things for the same reason: it is all about dreams and visions. The visions of the prophets are the visions of God Himself about the future of His creation, and He intends that these in turn should inspire us with dreams of our own. For the God we serve not only *was* the Creator; He *is* the Creator, renewing faith and hope, changing lives for the better, building His church, growing His kingdom. And since we were made in His image, we are most like Him when we are creating new things with Him – gaining new insights into the way He is and the way we are; developing our own potential; building new and better

31

relationships; changing the way we share the Good News to meet the changing needs of the world around us; as a church forever striving to come closer to being the kind of church He wants us to be.

But nothing new is possible without dreams and visions first. In fact, as King Solomon put it, *'where there is no vision, the people perish,'* and that's particularly true of your future church. Your future church needs to be different from any previous church, simply because it is called to serve a generation that is different from every other generation before it. For that reason alone, your present church must do some serious dreaming! And that dreaming (or 'visioning' as it's called now) can start with you. You have four excellent resources:

- ❧ The New Testament church to use as a basic model.
- ❧ Knowing what the Lord of the future has already told you through His prophets.
- ❧ Seeing the trends and developments in the world around you.
- ❧ Prayer.

With these resources you can begin to ask, 'What will my future church be like?' If you find that a difficult question to answer, remember the promise that Jesus has left on record, especially for twenty-first-century Christians like you:

'"Afterwards I will pour out my Spirit on everyone: your sons and daughters will proclaim my message; your old men will have dreams, and your young men will see visions. At that time I will pour out my spirit even on servants, both men and women . . . . But all who ask the Lord for help will be saved"'

That's a big promise if ever there was one! God has prom-

32

ised unprecedented blessings to equip His church for the unprecedented times ahead. His Spirit will use everyone who is willing to be used. And, if that is not enough, all of us, whoever we are, are privileged to be able to 'see', before they happen, the things He wants to achieve in saving men and women. And of course that includes the building of His future church. So let's claim the promise! Let's ask the Head of the church to tell us what we need to know. Let's pray: *'Lord, give me a vision of my future church.'*

It's unlikely that the Lord will answer your prayer with a dream or a vision such as He gave to Daniel. But as you think about it and use your imagination, He will begin to create a picture in your mind and a passion in your heart as He shares His plans for *His* future church with you. Ask Him to open your eyes to see the remarkable things He is doing in other churches. Hopefully, something you read in this book and other books like it will provide part of the answer. It will also help if you share your prayers and longings with others like yourself, and ask questions such as these:

- **What does it look like?** Is my future church growing? Is it a seventh-day church or a seven-days church? What are members doing for one another and their friends during the week, and how and where are they doing it? What does a typical Sabbath service look like, or aren't there any 'typical' services? Does the building that is used for church services look more like a church, or a centre of activity for the community? Does it have a stage or a platform, pews or chairs, and do they look comfortable or uncomfortable? What is happening in this church? Are lives being changed? Are believers growing?

- **Where is the centre** of my future church's life? Is it the sanctuary or the church hall, the pastor's office or the church members' homes? Is the church programme-centred or people-centred? Do the church's activities revolve around the pastor or elders, or does everyone have a say in what happens? Where is Jesus in the picture? Are unbelievers expected to come to where believers are in order to 'hear the message' or do believers meet with unbelievers where *they* are?

- **Who attends** this church? Who are the leaders and ministers – are they trained professionals or competent lay people? What is expected of the pastor, and what is expected of the members? Are the majority of worshippers young, middle-aged or elderly? Are they mostly church members or are there many visitors? How are the people dressed as they come and go? Which of my non-Christian friends can I see there? Who in particular is my church seeking to win for Christ?

- **What does it sound like** when the members of my future church get together? Is there mainly joy and celebration, or is the atmosphere quiet and serious? Is all the conversation religious, or are people sharing their lives with one another? How many languages are being spoken? Can the voices of children be heard? Is the music traditional or contemporary? Is there an organ or a piano, an orchestra or a band?

- **How does it feel** to be a part of my future church? Is it exciting or boring to be there? Is the church formal or informal, friendly or unfriendly, warm or cold? Is there a sense of freedom or control? Can I be myself or do I have to 'conform'? Do I feel accepted for who I am? Do I belong? Do I get the impression that other people love to be a part of this church, or are they there from a sense of duty? How flexible is it? Does it make changes easily or with difficulty?

- **Why does my future church exist?** Do the members of the church know? Are we there primarily for one another or for the people we want to win for Christ? If it's the latter, what is the church doing for the community and how is it making itself attractive and relevant to them?

God is going to give us many interesting answers to those questions. I say 'many' because one thing is certain: *your* future church is going to be different from *my* future church. Of course, as Christians and as Adventists we shall always hold certain unchangeable things in common about what we believe and how we live our lives. But how we express ourselves and live out our faith also has to be different in many ways. After all, a Christian congregation is not like a predictable equation in which a and b are constant and always equal c, but an unpredictable coming together of people and the Holy Spirit; and while the Holy Spirit Himself does not change, people do, and no two people are the same.

Perhaps in the past your church has not encouraged this kind of diversity within its unity as it might have done. While we have acted with the best intentions, perhaps we have stifled individuality and discouraged creativity. Perhaps we  have felt threatened by those who wanted to be different or do things differently from ourselves. We have confused unity with uniformity, in the mistaken belief that there is strength in everyone's doing the same thing in the same way. But I doubt that will be the case in your future church.

As we grow in Christ and find our security and assurance in Him, we won't be threatened by our differences. As the Spirit is permitted to use the gifts He has given believers, He will work powerfully through them to reach people His church has so far been unable to reach. As unique relationships grow among believers, and special ministries are developed for their friends, we can expect that God will raise up churches that are wonderfully different from one another, even though they may serve in the same city. Pastor Aris Vontzalides was right when he suggested (reverently, it should be said!) that the God we serve is a 'variety junkie'. He has created amazing variety in the natural world: it's only reasonable to expect the same sort of variety in His new world, the kingdom of the church, of which your future church will be an essential part.

Well, what does it look like? Is the picture you have of your future church crystal clear, and so exciting that the only thing to do is to share it with others and start turning the dream into reality? Or is the vision vague and blurred? If you are absolutely sure about what God wants you and your church to become, and you know how you are going to get from where you are to where you want to be, you probably don't need to read any further. But if you are like most of us, not content with the way the church is at the moment, but not sure about the way forward, read on.

None of us has all the answers, but we can grow in understanding together. In the following pages I should like to describe as best I can the vision of *my* future church. It has been taking shape in my mind's eye for several years now. Actually, it's a composite picture – a blending together of my own dreams, the ideas of others who dream about their own future church, and the realities of what God is actually doing now to build His church in various parts of the world. I must add that many details are still vague and uncertain, but I have no doubt that they will become clear as time goes by. So what follows are broad outlines and proven principles, which can be applied in all sorts of different ways to suit all sorts of different situations, including yours.

As you read, keep dreaming. And may your dreams come true!

---

[1] Proverbs 29:18 KJV.
[2] Joel 2:28, 29, 32.

Chapter Three

Apprentices Only

The challenge of discipleship

"'Go, then, to all peoples everywhere and make them my disciples.'"[1]

ave you ever had the feeling that when all is said
and done you don't know very much, either
about yourself and the world you live in, or about
God and the way He works? Do you ever feel
that you are going round in circles instead of actually going
somewhere with your life? Or, worse still, that you are going
backwards instead of forwards, down instead of up? That,
even after all your trying, you aren't exactly an outstanding
success in living the Christian life? Yet, in spite of everything, you're not giving up, you're going to keep following
Jesus, you want to learn from Him; you want to grow?
Welcome to the club! You qualify as a disciple. An apprentice.

This book is about your church and my church, and how we
believe the Lord of the church would like to see His church
develop in the future. As we know, however, churches can be
only what their members are, because the church is people.

Changing churches, changing lives

It stands to reason that our congregations will be open to
innovation, renewal and change in church life, only if they

are open to ongoing change and growth in their personal lives. Perhaps one of the reasons why the church as a whole is such a conservative institution is that too many Christians are more comfortable than they ought to be with the way they are. But if the first purpose of the Christian message is to make unbelievers comfortable with the good news of forgiveness and peace with God, its second purpose is to make believers feel *un*comfortable with the challenge of constant growth and change.

It's a familiar theme in the New Testament. The apostle Peter, for example, begins his second letter by encouraging us to develop one virtue after another, and closes with the admonition to *continue to grow* in grace and knowledge. Paul uses stronger words; to *'strive'*, *'run your best'* and *'abound more and more'* in growing towards godliness.[2] As for the spiritual gifts God has given us for service, we should *'set our hearts'* on obtaining the best gifts, while we develop the gifts we already have in order that our progress *'may be seen by all.'*[3]

A Lifelong Apprenticeship

When Jesus commissioned His disciples to go and make disciples, to whom was He talking, and what was He actually saying? Remember the setting? The resurrection was only forty days past, and then it was time for His return to heaven. He was ready to go, but what about His followers? Were they ready for what was coming next? I doubt it. Matthew says:

'The eleven disciples went to the hill in Galilee where Jesus had told them to go. When they saw him, they wor-

shipped him, even though some doubted. Jesus drew near and said to them, "I have been given all authority in heaven and on earth. Go, then, to all peoples everywhere and make them my disciples: baptize them in the name of the Father, the Son, and the Holy Spirit, and teach them to obey everything I have commanded you. And I will be with you always, to the end of the age." [4]

The eleven disciples were not the only ones at that meeting. *'The commission had been given to the twelve when Christ met with them in the upper chamber; but it was now to be given to a larger number. At the meeting on a mountain in Galilee, all the believers who could be called together were assembled . . . .*

'At the time appointed, about five hundred believers were collected in little knots on the mountainside . . . . Many who were present had never before seen Him.' [5]

The Gospel commission was given, then, not to a select few, but to all the believers, *including some who doubted.* But whether members of the inner circle or members of the multitude, they all had one thing in common. They were all ordinary people. A live interview for *News at Ten* would have revealed that without exception, all would have seen themselves as unprepared and unqualified to do what Jesus was asking them to do. At best, they would have seen themselves as apprentices. No problem: that's how Jesus saw them, too. Because that's what they were – apprentices. Disciples.

A disciple is an apprentice, someone who learns by following and watching a teacher, and then doing what he has seen the teacher do. Even now, especially in the area of manual skills, new employees may be contracted as apprentices for anything up to five years before they are given the responsibility of doing the job themselves without supervision. Discipleship – apprenticeship – is not just a Christian thing. What *is* unique about Christian discipleship, however, is that it's for life. Being a Christian involves a lifelong apprenticeship, a commitment to lifelong learning, development and growth. It starts the moment we choose Jesus as our life-Teacher, but it never ends.

The Gospel commission is all about finding people who are willing to learn from Jesus. Not people who already have everything together in their lives, but people who see themselves as beginners. And who is to do the finding? As we have already seen, that's the work of those who have already started their own apprenticeship. Disciples are commissioned to make disciples.

I find the idea both encouraging and daunting. I find it encouraging, because I see myself very much as an apprentice, and Jesus uses only apprentices to do this special work. I find it daunting, because, even after all these years, I seem to have further to go in my personal development now than I did at the beginning! But at least that confirms I'm on the right track. It's encouraging to know that *'The closer you come to Jesus, the more faulty you will appear in your own eyes; for your vision will be clearer, and your imperfections will be seen in broad and distinct contrast to His perfect nature. This is evidence that Satan's delusions have lost their power; that the vivifying influence of the Spirit of God is arousing you.'*[6]

Growing spiritually means . . .

. . . well, it obviously means more than there is room for here, but there is plenty of good reading material available on the subject for those who take their discipleship seriously.[7] It's all about discovering more fully the purpose of our existence, becoming the people God created us to be. Fortunately, it's never too late to start the journey. In brief, consider some of the ways Christian growth was understood by those who were among the first to follow Jesus.

- **Holistic growth.** Maybe you've heard about the T-shirt that was spotted at a political rally: *'Jesus save us . . . from your followers.'* Or perhaps you've heard about the way two girls describe their imaginary kingdom: *'It's like heaven only better – there aren't any Christians!'* [8] It's sad that Christians are often perceived as unbalanced, extremist, weird, and generally not very nice people to know, but sometimes it's hardly surprising. According to Paul, however, *'we must grow up **in every way** to Christ, who is the head'* (of the body). [9] Growing as Christians means growing more like Jesus, and He was no weirdo, even if He was revolutionary. We are encouraged to grow – holistically – as Jesus grew, *'both in body and in wisdom, gaining favour with God and men,'* [10] Understanding must grow with knowledge; grace must grow with wisdom; abilities must be developed with gifts; humility must grow with power.

  To put it more simply, look at life as Jesus did. According to Him, *everything* God has ever required of us is covered by just two basic principles, love for Him and love for one another. [11] So Christian growth could be summed up by a single, simple statement: learning to love.

  Christian counsellor Larry Crabb puts it this way:

'I believe it can be successfully argued that every personal or behavioural problem one might wish to change (e.g., bad

temper, perverted sexual desires, depression, anxiety, overeating) results ultimately from violations of the command to love.[12]

In my opinion that's where the challenge of Christian growth lies. 'Learning to love' may sound like a nice and simple idea, but it implies profound internal change, not just doing better but being different.

* **Stage-by-stage growth.** When we become members of God's family we are *'born again'*, and as *'newborn babies'* it's obvious we have some growing to do.[13] The disciple John often uses this analogy in his writings: in his first letter he specifically addresses three distinct, spiritual age-groups of people in the church – children, young men, and fathers.[14] Clearly, the church is a multi-generational family.

The point is, spiritual growth is normal; what is abnormal is not to grow. It's healthy to have spiritual children in the church, and it's best if their growth to spiritual maturity is gradual (crawling comes before walking, walking before running). So let's accept and provide for the fact that not everyone in the church is at the same stage of spiritual development. Those who are new to faith in Jesus should not feel guilty because they don't know everything the 'adults' in the church know. Those who are more spiritually mature must be gentle and patient with the spiritual babies, children, adolescents and youth around them. After all, we're all children in God's sight, and that's how He deals with us. How else could we cope with those periods of doubt and darkness that are part and parcel of growing in faith?

* **Painful growth.** From birth onwards, it seems life and

pain go together. Fortunately, the pain is usually more intermittent than constant, but 'growing pains' are normal. The fact is that growth of any kind means change, and change means pain. Growing in Christ from one stage to another is no exception. Following Jesus includes carrying a cross, remember? No one ever said it would be easy. What makes it difficult is that the pain of spiritual growth can come in unexpected ways.

One of my favourite Scripture verses is Isaiah 50:10. It's not an exaggeration to say that it 'came to me' just when I needed it most. During my first year of ministry I experienced what others have called the 'long dark night of the soul'. For no reason I could think of, except my own sinfulness, it seemed as if God had suddenly decided to terminate our relationship. He simply disappeared. Long periods of prayer didn't bring Him back; Bible study and church worship left me empty; even fasting made no difference. It was just as if someone had switched all the lights off, and I was left alone to find my way in the dark. And if that wasn't bad enough, there was another problem. How could I, a young pastor, lead others into an encounter with Christ if I was lost myself?

After several months of this I was close to giving up. Then one day while travelling on the London underground I pulled out my pocket Bible, let it fall open, and the only verse I saw on the page was Isaiah 50:10: *'All of you that honour the Lord and obey the words of his servant, the path you walk **may be dark indeed**, but trust in the Lord, rely on your God.'* (emphasis ours.)

You see why it's a favourite verse of mine. Jesus almost literally spoke to me *in the darkness*. It's a great reassurance to know that God is with us in the dark as well as in the light. It's also a great revelation to know that darkness

 is part of the experience of walking towards the light, that faith grows through doubt. And I must say, I prefer the life I have now, to what I had before that 'long dark night'. So if you find yourself questioning everything you once believed without question; if the God you once knew now seems remote and unknowable, don't despair. He has His own ways of leading you into a deeper, more mature relationship with Himself. Growing pains are part of growing up.

Growth in community. Paul's statement quoted above is made in the context of his exhortations about the need to build Christian community. He argues that the reason God has given spiritual gifts to every believer (i.e. every member of the body of Christ) is that as those gifts are developed and used in various forms of ministry, they benefit the entire church. *'And so shall we all come together to that oneness in our faith and in our knowledge of the Son of God; we shall become mature people, reaching to the very height of Christ's full stature.'*[15]

Again, the message is simple, yet not so simple. We grow together, in community, or we don't grow at all. Our personal growth is inseparably bound up with our relationships with other people.

Individualized growth. Having recognized the need for community to assist us in our individual growth, we also face the challenge of individualized growth. The fashion industry in its broadest form may determine the choice of music, clothes, hairstyle, car, language, and a hundred other things for millions of people, and threaten to make us more like sheep than human beings. But the fact remains that each of us is one-of-a-kind. We honour God as we develop our unique potential and move towards becoming the people we were created to be. God calls us to a *personal* relationship with Himself which in some ways will be different from His relationship with anyone else. Hence the new name He will give us one day. No one will know it except the One who gives it and the one who receives it.[16] Even in the great hereafter, it seems, we will all be different.

- **Never-ending growth.** The biggest challenge comes from the Master Himself. According to Jesus, there's only one goal for Christians: *'"You must be perfect – just as your Father in heaven is perfect!"'*[17] Fortunately, Jesus is not talking about the perfect keeping of many rules. As in so many of His teaching situations, He is talking about the only thing that really matters, love. Having said that, He *is* talking about loving our enemies, which means a major change in attitude, a profound internal change. He's also talking about loving as God loves, and that's hard for us to measure with our tiny little minds, let alone measure up to with our sin-damaged hearts.

A closer look at Jesus' words also makes it clear that Jesus is not describing an absolute, measurable standard which we shall one day be able to achieve, but an attitude which can constantly deepen and forever grow in the way it is expressed. Love is infinite as God is infinite. As far as our capacity to love is concerned, there will always be room for growth. As Philip Yancey says, *'One can never "arrive" in light of such sweeping commands as "Love the Lord your God with all your heart and with all your soul and with all your mind . . ."*[18] Perfection will always be in the future, because it is not a state arrived at but a state of becoming. For me, that is one of the attractions of heaven and eternity. It guarantees we'll never be bored.

How to Grow

Jesus once asked the rhetorical question: *'"Can any of you live a bit longer (or grow a bit taller) by worrying about it?"'*[19] There's nothing we can actually do to grow, either physically or spiritually. Growth takes place in living things provided they are healthy, and it's there that our responsibility lies. Just as we have to eat, exercise and rest to stay physically healthy, so there are things we can do to maintain our spiritual health. Some are fairly obvious, like Bible study, prayer, church attendance, obedience, and so on. But I think we need to be a bit more specific than that.

How we study the Bible is probably more important than the fact that we actually read the Bible. How we pray and how we participate in church life is probably more important than the fact that we actually do these things. Here are a few helpful principles I'm learning to apply. They challenge me; I hope they will challenge you.

🐾 **Accept responsibility for our own problems.** We have a tendency as Christians to blame the devil for everything, and in one sense that's right. Without him we wouldn't be in this mess. But blaming him – or anyone/anything else for that matter – for our failure to be all that we would like to be won't get us anywhere. Even if we did have a bad start in life, even if we are disadvantaged now, there comes a point when we have to take responsibility for our own lives and what we do with them.

🐾 **Admit we're helpless** to make all the changes we need to make in our lives. That sounds like a contradiction to the previous point, but it isn't. It's simply a matter of realizing that there are some changes we can make and some we can't. The fundamental changes we need to make in our lives are not superficial, external changes, but deep, internal ones. It's one thing to make changes in the food we eat or the way we keep Sabbath; it's another to change the way we are. For that kind of change, we are totally dependent on resources outside ourselves: God first of all, and the people He can use to minister to us. This kind of change or healing, more than physical healing, was what James had in mind when he wrote that believers would be healed as they confessed (i.e. admitted) their faults to and prayed for one another.[20]

◆ **Study Scripture relationally.** Simply knowing what the Bible says doesn't actually make any difference to our lives. In fact, it is possible to make a life-study of the Scriptures and still miss the message, as the Pharisees did. They *'searched the Scriptures'* as if they would be saved by doing so, and therefore saw no need to come to Jesus for life.[21] Information is important, of course. But application is even more important. Every time we study the Bible, we should ask not only, 'What is this Scripture saying and what does it mean?' but 'How does it apply to my life – what is God saying to me?' Relational Bible study challenges us constantly to face the fact of where we are in our relationship with God, and gives us something very specific to pray about.

◆ **Think 'outside the box'.** I once met a man who kept a small farm on the island of Jersey. At 70 years of age he was still doing what he had always done – growing potatoes and tomatoes. In all that time he had never left the island. The thought of travelling outside his valley, even to visit the main town of St Helier a short distance away, was something he entertained only when absolutely necessary. His world was about fifteen miles long by ten miles wide.

What about our world?

A few years ago J. B. Phillips wrote a book entitled *Your God is Too Small,* suggesting that Christians generally limit themselves by limiting their concept of God. As Adventists, we may also find it difficult to think 'outside the box' of our denominational teachings. But the world is bigger than we are, and God is infinite. Let us not be afraid to break out of that box by becoming *'thinkers, and not mere reflecters of other men's thought',* because *'every human being, created in the image of God, is endowed with a power akin to that of the Creator – individuality, power to think and to do.'*[22] We can challenge our own thinking by using new translations of the Bible and reading widely from Adventist and non-Adventist authors, but there is no substitute for simply thinking and prayerfully questioning everything. As Scott Peck puts it, if we dare to seek growth, we have to dare to think.[23]

- **Try new things.** Doing what we have always done is relatively easy, so why do anything different? We need to attempt new things because new things are difficult. They make us realize our limitations. They make us turn to God for His help and to our friends for support. Of course there is no point in trying to sing if you have no voice, but all of us have undeveloped potential somewhere. For example, if you enjoy giving Bible studies, you can learn to make them more affective by thinking of more penetrating questions and developing new outlines. Better still, you can develop your ability even further by teaching someone else to do the same. I realize this illustration is a 'doing,' external, thing, but it's surprising how doing new things helps us to know ourselves better, and brings deeper issues such as pride, fear, self-doubt, and laziness to the surface.

• **Find a mentor.** Jesus sent His first twelve on their missionary journeys in pairs, not only to encourage one another through the difficulties of missionary work, but to encourage and challenge one another in their personal lives. We also need at least one mature Christian friend to

do the same for us. For many of us our spouse may serve as our best critic, but ideally we need others with whom we can meet regularly to share our hopes and fears, others who will hold us accountable to our commitment to growth. Such people are more than just prayer partners: they are disciplers.

• **Be a mentor.** Many Christians find that the best motivation to spiritual growth is commitment to the spiritual growth of someone else who is either a 'pre-Christian' or a young Christian. If we can invite someone to '*imitate me . . . just as I imitate Christ*'[24] as Paul did, we are unlikely to become careless or apathetic in spiritual matters.

• **Join a small group.** As we have already observed, we grow in community or we really don't grow at all, because spiritual growth is all about learning to love; and love grows only as we live in community. A caring small group that encourages openness and honesty and provides a safe growing environment encourages holistic growth to take place. That includes growth in relationship with God, growth in relationship with others, and growth in service as gifts and talents are identified and developed. As Dale Galloway, pastor of a small-group church has observed: *'I believe that people grow at least eight times faster when they're in a small group and attending weekly worship/ celebration services on Sunday than if they just attended the service itself.'*[25]

◆ **Live by principles, not rules.** It's interesting to note that one of the first accusations Jesus faced was that He was breaking or abolishing the law by His teaching and example. His answer to His accusers is also significant: *'"Do not think that I have come to do away with the Law of Moses and the teachings of the prophets. I have not come to do away with them, but to make their teachings come true."'*[26] He then went on to show just how far-reaching the Ten Commandments are, that their application is not limited to actions but to thoughts and motives.

His way (the way of living by principle, or the spirit of the law) was clearly more demanding than their way (the way of living by the rules, or the letter of the law). It still is. Controlling the on/off switch is more difficult than dumping the television. Christian young people who have had the strictest upbringing usually have the biggest problems when they leave home for university, where they have to make all the decisions themselves. Living by principle is all about loving God, ourselves, and others (even enemies) in new as well as familiar situations. What we learned as children won't see us through as adults. We grow when we live by principles, not rules. We need the law in our hearts, not on tablets of stone. Leo Tolstoy illustrated it this way:

'A man who professes an external law is like someone standing in the light of a lantern fixed to a post. It is light all round him, but there is nowhere further for him to walk. A man who professes the teaching of Christ is like a man carrying a lantern before him on a long, or not so long, pole: the light is in front of him, always lighting up fresh ground and always encouraging him to walk further.'[27]

❧ **Dismantle the sacred/secular divide.** Which day is more sacred, Saturday or Monday? Whose work is the more important, the pastor's or the mother's? Where can we serve God better, in the church or in the workplace? Where is God more likely to be found, in the place of morning prayer or in the late-night club where a teenager is contemplating suicide?

There is no absolute answer to any of these questions, but the point is that spiritual growth doesn't happen in one small pigeon-hole of our lives, because the sacred is not limited to a small pigeon-hole of human experience. As C. S. Lewis has said, *'There is no neutral ground in the universe: every square inch, every split second is claimed by God and counterclaimed by Satan.'*[28] All our days belong to God, not just one. Our bodies are His temple, not a building made of brick. If our eyes and ears are open, we may meet Him anywhere, any time. And every meeting with Him will be a challenge to grow.

❧ **Be realistic.** Maybe I should have placed this first in the list rather than last, but it fits just as well here as anywhere, because unrealistic information and unrealistic expectations are just – unrealistic. In our pursuit of truth we have to start with who we are, and many never get past that point, because knowing the truth about ourselves is painful. But, after all is said and done, we are still who we are, a mixture of strength and weakness, good points and bad, divine presence and human nature.

Apparently Alcoholics Anonymous have a saying: *'I'm not okay, and you're not okay, but that's okay.'* It sounds like a healthy saying for Christians too. However much we might grow, when we look carefully at what we most deeply desire, we realize that what we want is simply not available, not until heaven. Let's do our individual best, help others along their way, allow for mistakes, and be realistic.

Church of Apprentices

Growth works both ways: churches grow as individual members grow, and individual members grow as their churches grow. Much of what follows in this book applies equally to individual growth and to the growth of the church as a whole. But it all hinges on our willingness to accept that the church is, first of all, people, individuals, apprentices. As Russell Burrill says, *'Having a discipleship strategy is absolutely essential if the church is interested in long-term maturity among its members.'*[29] In order to serve its apprentices well, I hope my future church will:

- **Place Discipleship before Membership.** The Gospel commission is to make disciples, not simply *'believers'* or church members. Church membership is important, but discipleship is more important. The strength of my future church depends more on the number of people regularly involved with the ministry and worship life of the church, whether they are fully-fledged Adventists or not, than the book membership of the church.

⛭ Establish a 'Discipleship Track' of some kind to ensure that new converts are provided with an on-going apprenticeship in the Christian life, for at least one year after they first come to faith in Christ. This training  period would involve a mentor – an *'experienced and trusted advisor'* [30] – who would meet weekly with the new disciple, to lead him or her from the initial conversion experience into a mature understanding and experience of the faith.

Rick Warren, in his classic work *The Purpose Driven Church,* [31] likens this process to a baseball diamond (like the square of a rounders pitch). The suggestion is that no one should be left at the starting point of either conversion or baptism, but that every new believer should circle the four bases. (And if we expect this of new believers, we should expect that every church member involved with those new believers should circle them too.) An Adventist version of the four bases could be as follows:

Base One: Acceptance of Jesus as Saviour and Lord, basic acquaintance with the twenty-seven fundamental doctrines, baptism and acceptance into church membership.

Base Two: The development of the discipline of a personal devotional life, including prayer, Bible study, and a meaningful, growing relationship with Jesus. Just because people accept Jesus and His teachings and agree to live a Christian lifestyle, does not necessarily mean that they have a solid devotional life. Research shows that many church members spend very little time in personal prayer or Bible study in between weekly church meetings.

Base Three: Discovery and development of spiritual gifts, and placement into ministry in harmony with those gifts.

Base Four: Training in witness, enabling the new disciple to become a disciple-maker.

⁂ **Establish a small-group network** as the basic unit of growth in the church, both for individual disciples and the community as a whole. The earlier new people can be encouraged to join a small group the better. The safety of a caring, small group makes it the best place for new believers to move along the discipleship track outlined above.

Growing disciples? No dream or vision of my future church can become a reality without them. With them, we can expect growing churches, churches which are altogether bigger and better than our churches of today.

---

[1] Matthew 28:19.

[2] 2 Peter 1:5-8; 3:18; 1 Timothy 6:11, 12; Philippians 1:9-11.

[3] 1 Corinthians 12:31; 1 Timothy 4:14, 15.

[4] Matthew 28:16-20.

[5] Ellen G. White, *The Desire of Ages*, pages 818, 819.

[6] Ellen G. White, *Steps to Christ,* pages 64, 65.

[7] Few books are better on this than *Steps to Christ,* especially the chapter, 'Growing Up Into Christ'. But if you are already familiar with this, try another small volume with a big impact which has blessed many Christians: *Inside Out* by Larry Crabb (Carlisle, UK: Paternoster Publishing, 1998).

[8] Quoted in Phillip Yancey, *The Jesus I Never Knew* (Great Britain: BCA, 1995), page 232.

[9] Ephesians 4:15, emphasis supplied.

[10] Luke 2:52.

[11] Matthew 22:37-40.

[12] *Inside Out,* page 43.

[13] There are at least seventeen references in the New Testament to the idea of being 'born' into the family of God, including the two quoted here, John 3:3; 1 Peter 2:2.

[14] 1 John 2:12-14.

[15] Ephesians 4:13.

[16] Revelation 2:17.

[17] Matthew 5:48. (Compare Luke 6:36 – ' "*Be merciful just as your Father is merciful.*" ')

[18] Philip Yancey, *What's So Amazing About Grace?* (Grand Rapids, Michigan: Zondervan, 1997), page 197.

[19] Luke 12:25 (see also Bible footnote).

[20] James 5:16.

[21] John 5:39.

[22] Ellen White had much to say on the importance of thinking for ourselves, and not being content for others (not even church leaders) to do our thinking for us. This particular quotation is made in the context of the purpose of *'true education'*. *Education*, page 17.

[23] M. Scott Peck, *The Road Less Travelled and Beyond* (London: Rider, 1997), page 47.

[24] 1 Corinthians 11:1.

[25] Dale Galloway, *The Small Group Book* (Grand Rapids, MI: Fleming H. Revell, 1995), page 69.

[26] Matthew 5:17.

[27] Quoted in Yancey, page 198.

[28] Quoted in Peck, *People of the Lie* (New York: Touchstone, 1998), page 83.

[29] *Rekindling a Lost Passion* (Fallbrook, California: Hart Research Center, 1999), page 201.

[30] *Oxford Dictionary.*

[31] Rick Warren, *The Purpose Driven Church: Growth Without Compromising Your Message and Mission* (Grand Rapids, MI: Zondervan, 1995), page 130.

Chapter Four

Bigger and Better

Aiming for growth and excellence

"'My thoughts,' says the Lord, "are not like yours, and my ways are different from yours. As high as the heavens are above the earth, so high are my ways and thoughts above yours."'[1]

S ome still think that 144,000[2] is the literal number of 'the remnant' who will be translated to heaven from among the living when Jesus comes again. So, with a membership of over twelve million, Seventh-day Adventists already have a serious problem! Why create a bigger problem by making the church bigger?

Big is beautiful. Or is it?

Fortunately, Jesus loves us too much to play the literal numbers game, and most of us accept that the saved who live to see Jesus come will be many more than 144,000. Nevertheless, we may still suffer from what we might call 'remnantitis', that affliction of the spirit that prevents us from seeing big things or think-

REMNANTITIS

ing big thoughts when we, think about our future church. A

remnant is a remnant after all, and remnants, by definition, have to be small.

But how small is small? Compared with a horse, a dog is small, but compared with a mouse, it's a giant. To the first 1,000 Adventists in Britain, our present membership of 20,000 would have seemed a huge and unreachable goal. Compared to the present population of 56 million, however, 20,000 is miniscule: we are outnumbered 2,800 to one, almost too insignificant to count. Against such a population, even a million Adventists would still be a remnant, a number we could get away with if we had a problem with bigness. Have we dishonoured God and limited our growth by our small thinking?

A certain pastor was convinced that the limited success of his ministry was due to the absence of the power of God in his life. So he began to pray for more power. Day after day, he would fall to his knees and beg and plead with God to fill him with power for his work, and day after day he felt as powerless as ever. Finally in desperation, he cried aloud: 'Lord, why don't you answer my prayer? Why don't You fill me with Your power?' And at last the answer came: 'My son, with plans as small as yours, you don't need My power.'

Many things can limit a church's numerical growth, of course, but failure to dream BIG dreams and see God-sized visions are definitely factors. Allow your mind to be stretched by considering the following:

* Even in the golden pioneer days of the Advent movement, the church was told that *'if men in humble life were encouraged to do all the good they could do, if restraining hands were not laid upon them to repress their zeal, there would be **a hundred workers for Christ where now there is one.'**[3]* It was about that same time that another familiar challenge was heard, that *'if we would humble ourselves*

*before God, and be kind and courteous and tenderhearted and pitiful, there would be **one hundred conversions to the truth where now there is only one.**'[4]* So a larger work is possible. It isn't just a dream.

* A larger work is not just a possibility: the Lord of the harvest intends to make it a reality. We have the assurance that *'the great work of the gospel is not to close with less manifestation of the power of God than marked its opening . . . . Now the rays of light penetrate everywhere, the truth is seen in its clearness, and the honest children of God sever the bands which have held them . . . . Notwithstanding the agencies combined against the truth, a large number take their stand upon the Lord's side.'[5]*

* In 1905 Ellen White[6] stated that the time would come when as many would be converted in a day as there were on the day of Pentecost. At our present rate of growth around the world, some would say we are not far away from reaching that number. But Ellen White was not speaking of the overall growth of the church. She was speaking specifically about the Jewish people. In other words, as many *Jews* would be converted in a day as were converted at Pentecost. And she went on to say that Jewish people would be used mightily by God in the finishing of His work. Is there a Jewish community near your church? If so, what can your church do now to be ready when the big day arrives?

* Something is happening! Many Adventist and other Christian observers share a growing conviction that God's Spirit is now moving everywhere and stirring the church in a way we have not seen before. You could call it a 'divine

restlessness' that is making Christians long for the church to be bigger and better than it is at present. Evangelistic zeal, and interest and belief in the Second Coming of Jesus are now found throughout the Christian church – a far cry from a few years ago, when it seemed that only Adventists and a few other Christian groups cared about evangelism or believed in the Second Advent.

- More people are becoming Christians now than ever before. Despite the news to the contrary, there is a world-wide reawakening to spirituality taking place, which includes Europe and Great Britain. It's true than many churches are declining and dying, but others are growing in an almost unprecedented way. Through small groups and the cell church movement especially, the Bible is being studied and shared more widely and personally than ever. Estimates suggest that one million people in Britain are involved in small groups. In the USA the number is close to fifteen million.

- What or who is behind the computer and communications revolution of the last few years? Information of all kinds can now, for the very first time in history, be communicated to the large majority of the world's population simultaneously and in a matter of minutes Is that good or bad? Was it all down to man's ingenuity? Was it the enemy who developed today's incredible machinery as a way of corrupting Earth's inhabitants and taking as many as possible to destruction with him? Or was it our heavenly Father who loves every last person on Earth, and desperately wants to communicate His longing to have His children home?

- This is the age of youth. Whether the rest of us like it or not, it is youth culture that largely determines what goes and what doesn't. Young people have a voice, both in the community and in the church, which they never had before. Young people are managing directors, politicians, television news-readers, film stars, sports heroes – and evangelists. Is this the time Ellen White was referring to when she wrote that *'with such an army of workers as our youth, rightly trained, might furnish, how soon the message of a crucified, risen and soon-coming Saviour might be carried to the whole world!'*[7]

I get the distinct impression that my future church needs to be bigger, in every way, than it is now! Bigger in membership, more large-hearted, able to communicate with more and different people in the community. But it not only needs to be bigger – it also needs to be better.

Notice the Lampshades

It's so easy to get used to mediocrity. When the same people attend the same church week after week; when they do the same things and sing the same hymns Sabbath after Sabbath, they may fail to notice certain things which, to visitors, stand out like sore thumbs. Such as broken lampshades, for example.

When I arrived to serve a certain church for the first time,

I received a warm welcome and enjoyed the fellowship. But what made the biggest impression were the broken lampshades. Of the eight lampshades which adorned the sanctuary, three were

broken (all were dirty). My observation took the senior deacon by surprise. The lampshades had been like that for so long, that no one noticed them any more!

Maybe you think this was a petty issue. But visitors to our churches do notice things like these, and two in particular. Research has shown that poor-quality church bulletins and soiled toilets are more likely to cause visitors to have a negative first impression of the church as a whole, than anything else. My future church, and I hope yours, too, will take care of the 'lampshades'. It will have an attractive, informative bulletin that tells visitors all they need to know; and it will have clean toilets that are kept clean for the duration of the Sabbath programme.

But just a caution here. It's no use investing time and money in toilets and bulletins if what they represent is also mediocre. I see my future church aiming towards excellence in everything. I realize that none of us gets all of it right all of the time, but what we do and how we do it should reflect, as far as possible, the importance of our mission and the perfection of the One we serve. At least we should try to identify the various 'broken lampshades' in our churches, and do something about putting them right. How about the following for starters, just in the area of church meetings:

- **Messy meetings.** It's obvious to any visitor in this kind of meeting that even if the individual parts of the meeting are good, no thought has been given to how they fit together. There is no 'flow' to the service. It just consists of many unrelated bits and pieces. A well-chosen worship committee[8] can help to put this right, whenever possible bringing together beforehand all those taking part to plan the service as a co-ordinated whole.

- **Unprepared participants.** Even if the worship service,

Sabbath school, small-group, AYS or evangelistic meeting has been well planned, it's no good if it appears to the congregation that the preacher only pre-pared his sermon on the way to church, or the per-

DON'T LISTEN TO MY VOICE JUST LISTEN TO THE WORDS!

son appointed to lead in prayer gave first thought to it while singing the opening hymn. Church services and activities need to be planned well ahead of time, and all those taking part need to be well prepared.

❧ **Painful preliminaries.** When the welcome and announce-ments take half an hour, something has to be wrong! When there is so much 'special music' or promotion of church activities that the preacher begins to preach when the serv-ice ought to close, perhaps our priorities are not quite right. In my humble opinion, there should be no 'prelimi-naries' at all in our church services – if they cannot be made part of the worship service itself, they should be omitted altogether.

❧ **Incredible introductions.** Sometimes the introductions given to the platform party and speaker are worthy of the arrival of the Queen of Sheba. But when we gather to wor-ship let's remember we have not come to see a celebrity; we have come to worship God, and in His presence we are all on level ground. Short and simple introductions are best, and there is no need to recognize 'special' visitors such as church leaders in the congregation as if they are more important than our friends and relatives.

❧ **Insensitive instrumentalists.** I know what the Bible says about making a joyful noise before the Lord, but when I

can't hear myself think because the drummer is having such a good time, or the organist would do the congregation a favour by letting them sing unaccompanied, we're taking the text too far. More than anything else, the quality of the music used by a church affects our experience of worship. Better to use CDs or other pre-recorded music to sing with than to use musicians and/or song leaders who cause the rest of us pain or embarrassment – or both!

<ul>
<li>Marketplace mindset. I see my future church as a happy church in which every member is conscious of the freedom there is in Christ. But I don't want my future church to be disorderly, distracting and disrespectful. I can't expect my unchurched friends to understand why people wander in and out of the place of worship or conduct their conversations while the Bible is being read or a saxophone solo is being played, if I can't understand it myself.</li>
</ul>

You probably have your own pet grievances about the less-than-excellent way some things happen in your church, and I'm not suggesting that we all become petty super-critics of one another. But if you are aware of some badly-broken 'lampshades', please find a way, in the spirit of Christ, to get them fixed. We have some growing to do, and growing up is what being disciples of Jesus is all about. My future church has to be bigger – and better – than it is now. Visitors to my future church should be able to say as they leave, 'That was really excellent.' Because then I know they will be back for more.

[1] Isaiah 55:8, 9.

[2] Revelation 7:4; 14:1.

[3] Ellen G. White, *The Desire of Ages,* page 251 (emphasis ours).

[4] Ellen G. White, *Testimonies,* vol. 9, page 189.

[5] Ellen G. White, *The Great Controversy*, pages 611, 612.

[6] Article, 'The Need of Home Religion', *Review and Herald* (Washington D.C.: Review and Herald Publishing Co., 29 June 1905). The original statement was made by Mrs White in a talk given at the General Conference session on 27 May 1905.

[7] Ellen G. White, *Education,* page 271.

[8] See Appendix A for more on the makeup and role of the worship committee.

Chapter Five

Hole Truth or Whole Truth?

The true church must be truth-full

'I may have the gift of inspired preaching; I may have all knowledge and understand all secrets; I may have all the faith needed to move mountains – but if I have no love, I am nothing.'[1]

What *is* truth? Have you found the answer to that question yet? It's not as simple as it sounds, is it? As Adventists we sometimes say we have the truth; but is that really true? Do we understand the truth we *do* have without error? Do our twenty-seven fundamental beliefs embrace all the truth there is? You know the answers to those questions. Like the mint with the hole, there could be more.

In his fascinating book, *The Ragamuffin Gospel*, Brennan Manning quotes Jean Danielou's assertion that *'truth consists in the mind giving to things the importance they have in reality.'* He then adds, *'The really real is God.'[2]* God Himself is the ultimate and absolute truth. That being true, we have a long way to go, both in our understanding of the truth and in our practice of it, as Ellen White frequently observed.[3]

Fortunately, we have all eternity to explore the infinity of the truth of God.

It is this same great fact which makes the life of a disciple of Jesus so profoundly challenging. Jesus, because of who He was, rightly claimed, *'I am the way, the truth, and the life.'* No other significant religious leader has ever made such a statement about himself or herself. Christianity is the only faith which equates truth with a person. 'Accepting the truth,' therefore, is far more than gaining an understanding of and giving verbal assent to a set of neatly formulated doctrines or teachings, however helpful they may be in themselves. Accepting the truth means following Jesus, and following Jesus is a matter of accepting and coming to terms with *everything* that He stands for as we grow in personal relationship with Him. Consequently we may be far closer to the truth if we decide with Paul that we will *'forget everything except Jesus Christ and especially his death on the cross'*[4] than if we insist that 'the truth' consists only of twenty-seven doctrinal statements. Those statements are true, but they neither embrace all that is true about Jesus, nor all that we can know and experience in relationship with Him.[5]

The Truth Behind the Truth

This is not to say that the doctrines are not important. Of course they are important. The question is, of what value are the doctrines of the church, without the truth behind the doctrines? Without a doubt, from the beginning our church has been a message-driven church. Our God-given understanding of past, present and future is what has brought us to where we are today. But are we satisfied with where we are? Are *you* satisfied? If you were, you probably wouldn't be reading this and thinking about your future church.

Personally, I see my future church as going beyond where

we are today, both in understanding and in the practice of the truth. For that to happen, my future church must have not only clearly defined doctrines or teachings; it must comprehend, perhaps better than we have comprehended in the past, the truth that undergirds these doctrines. The message may drive the church, but what drives the message? The answer is found in the world's favourite Scripture: *'God loved the world so much that he gave his only Son.'*[6]

Here, two great truths about God are made clear. First, God loves unconditionally; and second, He gives unreservedly. Surely, therefore, those two facts should also be as much a part of our church's identity as are our twenty-seven fundamental beliefs? In fact, Paul's frequently-used argument, stated in the verses quoted at the beginning of this chapter, is that we may 'know' Scripture and proclaim it with passion, but if love doesn't saturate the message and drive the proclamation of it, it counts for absolutely nothing.

How important, then, that we give proper place to these larger truths behind the smaller truths, and that our church – my future church and hopefully yours – is known for the values and principles it stands for, not just 'the message'. It must be a truth-driven, not just a message-driven church. It is this personalization of the truth in Jesus that is the source of the power of the Christian message. As He explained in two related statements He made to the Pharisees:

'"If you obey my teaching, you will know the truth, and the truth will set you free."'

'"If the Son sets you free, then you will be really free."'[7]

The religion of the Pharisees as it was in the time of Jesus was defined and confined by rigid statements of belief and detailed rules and regulations. Unfortunately, they knew the letter of the law well, but were strangers to the spirit of the law. Because *'the written law brings death, but the Spirit gives life',*[8] the common people were drawn to Jesus as they found new life and wonderful liberty in following Him, even though His way demanded far more than the way of the Pharisees. And the same should be true today.

A Values Statement?

It is significant that the few sermons of Jesus we have on record have more to do with life values than doctrinal teachings. While Jesus clearly taught doctrinal truth (the state of the dead, the second advent, the Sabbath, etc.) His first concern seems to have been the values which reflect the character of God, undergird relationships and build community. In fact the failure of the religious leaders to understand their importance was the cause of the most scathing rebuke He ever uttered. They (quite rightly) paid their tithes to the last leaf of a garden herb, but they neglected *'to obey the really important teachings of the law such as justice, mercy and honesty'* which was about the same as straining a fly out of their drink but swallowing a camel![9]

The famous Sermon on the Mount was really Christ's defining statement about the Kingdom of God. It describes what the King and the citizens of the kingdom are, or should be, like, and how they should relate with each other. While it includes references to the law, marriage, prayer, fasting, heaven and stewardship (among other subjects), the heart of the sermon is about motives and attitudes, the driving forces of the Kingdom. Humility, mercy, purity, childlike trust in God, and love for one's enemies are the true marks of those who make up the kingdom of heaven on Earth, not simply the ability to recite or observe the external requirements of the law. Most of the parables of Jesus make the same point.

If kingdom values were important to Jesus, should they not be equally important to us? If Jesus saw the need to 'spell them out', should we not do the same, for our own sake as well as for the sake of those who request baptism and membership of our churches? So why don't we? Why not raise the subject at a church board meeting, or even a Sabbath school class or small-group meeting, and try to agree on the values which are most important to the life of your church? And then teach those values as you would teach the doctrines. Your list might look something like those in the box above, but it should be tailor-made to fit the needs of your church.

The Value of Values

Values challenge the heart, not just the mind. Values determine how we live, and have the power to change other lives. As Paul once observed, it is the goodness of God that leads to repentance.[10] Values likewise shape and drive the local church, and determine what it will feel like for visitors who worship there. They probably determine whether young people growing up in the church will stay or leave. They also determine whether or not kingdom growth is taking place in the church. Just because more people are attending church services and giving more offerings, it does not necessarily mean that the growth God values is taking place.

Values of Truth

From an evangelistic point of view, it is important to notice that congregations which are making the greatest impact on their communities are those which emphasize Christian values as well as Christian doctrine. Christian Schwartz found in his world-wide survey[11] that all churches experiencing outstanding growth share eight common characteristics or values, regardless of their doctrinal or cultural differences. In other words, whether churches were Protestant or Catholic, charismatic or conservative, Developing world or Developed world, they were likely to be growing if the eight characteristics were central to their life.

No wonder then that Schwartz's work is being taken seriously by Seventh-day Adventists. The fourth and largest-ever annual *'Seeds'* church planting summit organized by the North American Division Evangelism Institute and held at Andrews University in June 1999 was based entirely on the development of the eight characteristics in Adventist churches.

You may be wondering at this point what the connection is between the title of this chapter and the characteristics of growing churches. The connection is simply that they tend to make the reality or truth of God available and meaningful in practical ways to the people He loves. This is why some prefer to call them 'values' – they are valuable or essential in the living of the Christian life, and therefore the life of the church, as Jesus first modelled it. Consider Schwartz's eight values briefly:

1. Empowering leadership
Whereas Lucifer's ambition is to gather power to himself

71

and become like God, Christ's ambition is to enable others to become all that they were created to be. True Christian leadership is therefore all about assisting individual Christians to attain their potential as ministers of Christ. This is rather different from the idea of Christian leaders' *using* lay workers to help them achieve their own goals and pursue their own ministry.

2. Gift-oriented lay ministry

This value recognizes that believers serve best when they serve according to the spiritual gifts they have been given, not just the talents they possess or the skills they have developed. Skills and talents are useful in the performance of tasks, but only spiritual gifts are useful in the work of changing lives. Unless church leaders and committees understand this, they are in danger of putting square pegs in round holes when appointing members to church office. In practical terms this means, for example, that it makes no sense to appoint individuals to teach the Sabbath school class if they do not have the spiritual giftedness to do so.

3. Passionate spirituality

God does not save us out of a sense of duty, but because He feels deeply for the well-being of His children. He wants to communicate that concern through His church. Therefore a church *'can hardly expect to experience growth, as long as its members do not learn to live their faith with contagious enthusiasm and to share this faith with others.'*[12]

4. Functional structures

The actual life and death of Jesus was far more functional in changing lives and reconciling men and women to God than the Old Testament ceremonial system which foreshadowed it. For this reason, the ceremonial system was abolished at the cross. In the same way, churches must cease using programmes which have long since passed their sell-by date, and dismantle committees and departments which no longer serve their original purpose well. They must stream-line the way they use their energies and resources, in order to communicate the Gospel and serve the community in the most efficient and effective way.

5. Inspiring worship services

Just as joyful worship is the very atmosphere of heaven, so the spirit of worship will permeate the church in which believers not only talk about God but experience Him. Such worship speaks well of Him and makes His service attractive to others.

6. Holistic small groups

Interestingly, Schwartz's survey identifies the single most important characteristic of the eight as *'the multiplication of small groups,'*[13] and not without good reason. God's nature is love, because for eternity He has existed within the intimate community of the Trinity. On the level of human experience, He is best able to communicate His love through small groups of people whose oneness reflects His own and who genuinely care for one another.

7. Need-oriented evangelism

Throughout the Bible story, God is always the God who meets His people where they are, at a point of felt need. Christ's approach to ministry was the same, demonstrating His care by approaching different people differently and treating them as individuals, rather than using one approach for all as if they were numbers. Evangelism today is proving most successful where its purpose is to address human need and answer the questions people are asking, rather than to prove certain points of doctrine.

8. Loving relationships

As Schwartz observes, *'unfeigned, practical love has a divinely generated magnetic power far more effective than evangelistic programmes which depend almost entirely on verbal communication.'*[14] Created in God's image, people were made for such relationships. Without them, they are not fully human. Churches where such relationships are intentionally encouraged and developed through small groups will naturally be attractive to believers and unbelievers alike. Loving relationships make the truth real as nothing else can.

The true church

Most of us understand by now that any claim we make to belong to the true church must be based on something more than a 'proof of membership' baptismal certificate. Likewise, our identity as 'the remnant church' must be founded on something more than our history as a movement. Only as a church fulfils the divine purpose or mission which brought it into existence can it continue to be a genuine church, regardless of what it claims for itself.

The Bible's description of God's people who live in the period just prior to Christ's return is simple but far-reaching: *'Those who obey God's commandments and are faithful to Jesus'*[15] This obviously includes the Ten Commandments and the things which Jesus believed. But it surely goes beyond that. Jesus has also commanded us to love one another, and to go and make disciples (among other things).[16] It follows that a church which is not a missionary church is disqualified from calling itself a church, remnant or otherwise. Similarly, a congregation which is not a genuinely loving community is not really a church either – by definition!

According to market research specialist and consultant George Barna, the only churches which qualify as authentic churches of Christ are those which are built on six essential 'pillars': worship, evangelism, service, education and training, building community, and stewardship.[17] Clearly, my church needs to build on these pillars if it is to have a future. It also needs to embrace some or all of the 'truth values' defined by Schwartz, above, and possibly add others which its members agree are vital to its growth and ministry.

I find it personally challenging and encouraging to see what other churches and movements have done or are doing in this respect, and how they are growing as a result. I think we can learn from them, so I include just two examples in summary form here.

Example A: Cell Church UK. This organization is a branch of an international cell-church movement embracing congregations of various denominations which aspire to the cell model of church. Doctrines may differ, but values are shared. In their quarterly journal[18] they display seven key values as follows:

- **Jesus at the centre.** Meeting with Jesus at core. Only Jesus changes people.
- **Every member in ministry.** Every member feeling he has a ministry and role key to revival.
- **Every member growing.** Every person taking responsibility for his personal holiness and growth in his walk with Christ.
- **Multiplication.** The spreading of the Gospel and making of disciples at the heart of cells.
- **Sacrificial love.** Jesus demonstrated love by sacrifice. His

love is the challenge to us all.

- ☙ **Community.** The building of relationships both within and without the cell produces community.
- ☙ **Honesty.** Honesty is the lifeblood of community and the doorway to Christian growth.

Example B: Willow Creek Community Church, Chicago. Most Adventists in the Western World are familiar with this remarkable church, which has inspired thousands of congregations to become more relevant to modern people, more evangelistic, and more user-friendly. We, too, can learn something from a congregation of fourteen thousand which wins over one thousand unchurched people to Christ each year. Senior pastor Bill Hybels lists ten 'beliefs' which have been vital to the effective ministry of this church:[19]

- ☙ **Anointed teaching.** We believe that anointed teaching is the primary catalyst for transformation in the lives of individuals and in the church.
- ☙ **Lost people matter.** We believe that lost people matter to God and therefore ought to matter to the church.
- ☙ **Cultural relevance.** We believe that the church should be culturally relevant, while remaining doctrinally pure.
- ☙ **Authenticity.** We believe that Christ's followers should manifest authenticity and yearn for continuous growth.
- ☙ **Gifts-based ministry.** We believe that the church should operate as a unified community of servants stewarding their spiritual gifts.
- ☙ **Loving relationships.** We believe that loving relationships should permeate every aspect of church life.
- ☙ **Small-group ministry.** We believe that life change happens best in small groups.
- ☙ **Excellence.** We believe that excellence honours God and inspires people.

- **Gifted leadership.** We believe that churches should be led by those with leadership gifts.
- **Fully devoted followers.** We believe that full devotion to Christ and His cause is normal for every believer.

Like me, you might in the past have been tempted to think that the reason other churches grew more quickly than we did was because it was harder to be an Adventist than 'just a Christian'. May we be forgiven! Some of the world's fastest-growing churches make larger demands and require greater commitment of their members than we do. Look again at the values and beliefs just listed. The members in your present church may all keep the Sabbath on Saturday and pay their tithe, but do they all obey the truth behind the truth as it is in Jesus?

Living the Truth

Obviously, the church is only what its members make it. We *are* the church: so we have to ask what it means to live the truth in our personal lives For some, it simply means 'not telling lies' or 'telling the truth' as we have been taught to do in school or at home. If it was you who broke the window, admit it and take the consequences – don't blame someone else. For others, it means brutal honesty, usually about someone else's failings. It means 'telling it as it is' with all guns blazing – regardless of the damage that might do to the other person's feelings or reputation. How many would-be disciples have been permanently put off the church by the desperate desire of a well-meaning but ruthless church member to 'get to the Sabbath' or to point out that good Adventists don't wear jewellery? Too many, I'm afraid.

You may not believe this, but it's true. I knew a church elder some years ago who claimed that he had 'witnessed' to

 every home in his town. His method was simple. After an opening greeting he would unroll a chart listing the Ten Commandments, and ask the person at the door if he kept all ten, including the Saturday Sabbath. When the answer was 'no', he would unroll a second chart representing the seven last plagues and explain that the plagues would fall on the person if he didn't accept 'the truth'. Was he being truthful? Possibly. Was he witnessing to the truth? Absolutely not! And surprise, surprise, he didn't win any converts to the truth, either.

Living the truth is more than not telling lies or passing on a message, even if the message is about Jesus. And we can't sum it up by saying that it means being like Jesus, either. True, that's the goal, but we've already noticed that being like Jesus is like going on a journey and never getting to the destination, because Jesus is God and God is infinite, and He has given us eternity to become like Him. No, living the truth here and now is a bit closer to home. The 'truth' is not just about God; it's about ourselves.

In terms of worldly wisdom, the opposite of truth is error. In terms of God's wisdom, the opposite of truth is untruth. It's not just telling a lie, but living a lie. While God is the ultimate Truth and Jesus the personal representation of that Truth to us, notice how the great adversary to the Truth is represented as the father of lies:

'"*From the very beginning he was a murderer and has never been on the side of truth, because there is no truth in him. When he tells a lie, he is only doing what is natural to him, because he is a liar and the father of all lies. But I tell the truth, and that is why you do not believe me."*,[20]

The devil's murderous intentions grew out of his inability to live with the truth of God. He wanted something that he couldn't have (worship); so he pretended to be something he wasn't (equal with God). For the same reason, the Pharisees' attempt to murder Jesus on this occasion[21] grew out of their inability to be at peace in His presence. They wanted something they didn't deserve (respect); so they pretended to be something they weren't (more holy than other people).

It was not just Christ's teaching about His own unique relationship to God that upset them, even though they understood His claims to be blasphemous and worthy of death. The truth that was so distasteful to the Pharisees was the way His very presence revealed the truth about themselves, that is, their own falsehood. They belonged to the same group of men, remember, who had hoped to accuse Jesus (falsely) by bringing to Him a woman caught in an adulterous act, which they themselves had set up. They were well aware of the embarrassment Jesus had caused when He had revealed His knowledge of their own sinful secrets by writing about them in the dust beside the trembling body of that terrified woman.

What today's churches and professing Christians must not miss about this story is that the promise of freedom was offered specifically to those Pharisees who believed in Him (or 'on' Him).[22] They were impressed by what they had already seen and heard. Christ's words had struck an answering chord in their hearts and they were *'drawn to Him in faith'.*[23] But apparently they were willing to go so far and no further. They were unwilling to admit that they were still in bondage and needed to be liberated from anything. They were deeply offended by the idea that only by becoming disciples of this humble Galilean could they find real freedom.

That kind of self-surrender, which meant admitting the truth about themselves to both God and men was a sacrifice they were not prepared to make. So, although Jesus acknowledged that they were descendants of Abraham in one sense, the truth was that for all practical purposes they were still the devil's children. He called them actors,[24] pretenders or liars who claimed to be something they are not. Such living a lie results in the worst kind of bondage, for it is bondage from which there can be no deliverance, no salvation.

Where do you see yourself and your church in this story? Are you also guilty of living a lie? It's quite possible. This age more than any other is an age of pretence, in which trivia is clothed with glitter and people have been seduced away from what is real. Pop stars, film producers and sports heroes probably have more say in setting society's standards and priorities than do religious leaders, politicians or university professors. Looking good and feeling good is becoming more important than being good. Image is everything. Even for Christians. Even for churches.

Seventh-day Adventists, probably more than most Christians, can easily fall into the same trap as the Pharisees did. We have a carefully thought through list of beliefs, as they did. We expect church members to comply with a set of life-style standards concerning dress, deportment, diet, and leisure activities, as they did. Just as they had a mental picture of the *'good Pharisee'*, we know what a *'good Seventh-*

day Adventist' should look like, sound like, and even smell like. And just as they wanted society to think well of them, so we want people to think well of us.

The question is, how do we create and maintain that personal and corporate image? By doing things Christ's way or the way of the deceiver? As we have already seen, it's possible to begin by following one and end up following the other. Like the evil one, the great illusionist, do we make false claims about ourselves or the church? Do we sometimes exaggerate our achievements and falsify our true condition? Or, like Jesus, do we live the truth? It's an honest question, and if we're not prepared to give an honest answer, the only people we shall be fooling will be ourselves. As Brennan Manning points out:

'At (Sabbath) worship, as in every dimension of our existence, many of us pretend to believe we are sinners. Consequently, all we can do is pretend to believe we have been forgiven. As a result, our whole spiritual life is pseudo-repentance and pseudo-bliss.'[25]

If individual Christians are capable of such pretence, the church is as well. And the consequences of 'living a lie' will be the same for churches as for individuals – isolation from the real world. Theologian Dietrich Bonhoeffer wrote as passionately as anyone about the need for churches to 'get real' and for Christians to live the truth with each other. Consider this:

'He who is alone with his sins is utterly alone. It may be that Christians, notwithstanding corporate worship, common prayer, and all their fellowship in service, may still be left to their loneliness. The final breakthrough to fellowship does not occur because, though they have fellowship with one another as believers and as devout people, they do not have

fellowship as the undevout, as sinners. The pious fellowship permits no-one to be a sinner. So everyone must conceal his sin from himself and from their fellowship. We dare not be sinners. Many Christians are unthinkably horrified when a real sinner is discovered among the righteous. So we remain alone with our sin, living in lies and hypocrisy. The fact is that we are sinners!'[26]

Not much has changed since those words were written, either in human nature or in the church. Just as it is the hardest thing for individuals to admit to their utter sinfulness and their desperate need of grace, so it is painful for a community of Christians to admit their corporate failures openly. It's much nicer to report membership gains

than losses, or opening new churches than closing old ones. Triumphalism comes much more easily to us than realism. We like to feel good about ourselves and look good to others. But while glowing reports may create a temporary feel-good factor, if they are less than the truth they will result in disillusionment, and many who are seeking the truth will look elsewhere for it.

We need to accept the truth, not only about God but about ourselves, and then begin to live the truth. Not that there's anything to fear in that, since it's the truth that gives us what we always hoped for anyway, including the freedom to be ourselves without the need to pretend. As Eugene Petersen says it so well in his unique translation of Romans 5:2:

'We throw open our doors to God and discover at the same moment that he has already thrown open His door to us. We

82

find ourselves standing where we always hoped we might stand – out in the wide open spaces of God's grace and glory, standing tall and shouting our praise.'[27]

My future church must be truth-driven in the fullest sense of the word. And that shouldn't prove so difficult, if we can just change our definition of truth from propositions to persons – God Himself, first of all, then the men, women and children who give meaning to our lives – and how it is that Christ can bring us all together.

---

[1] 1 Corinthians 13:2.

[2] Quoted in Brennan Manning, *The Ragamuffin Gospel* (Oregon, U.S.A.: Multnomah Books, 1990), page 134.

[3] For example: '*God requires of them (His true people) continual advancement in the knowledge of the truth, and in the way of holiness.*' White, *Testimonies*, vol. 5, page 345.

[4] 1 Corinthians 2:2.

[5] W. Floyd Bresee, in *Seventh-day Adventists Believe* (Hagerstown, MD, U.S.A.: Review and Herald, 1988) explains that the book was written '*to reveal how Seventh day Adventists perceive God*' and '*to share our vision of Christ.*' Not surprisingly, he adds this significant statement: '*Recognising that He who is the incarnation of truth is infinite, we humbly confess that there is still much truth to be discovered.*' Page vii.

[6] John 3:16.

[7] John 8:32, 36.

[8] 2 Corinthians 3:6.

[9] Matthew 23:23.

[10] Romans 2:4.

[11] Christian A. Schwartz, *Natural Church Development* (Moggerhanger, Beds, UK. British Church Growth Association, 1996).

[12] ibid, page 27.

[13] ibid, page 33.

[14] ibid, page 36.

[15] Revelation 14:12

[16] John 13:34; Matthew 28:19.

[17] ibid, page 89.

[18] *Cell Church U.K.* (Harpenden, Herts, England: Cell Church UK).

[19] These values are listed and developed in detail in Lynne and Bill Hybels, *Rediscovering Church* (Grand Rapids, MI: Zondervan Publishing House, 1995),

pages 183-194.

[20] John 8:44b, 45.

[21] Verses 37, 40, 59.

[22] Verse 30, 31.

[23] Ellen G. White, *The Desire of Ages,* page 466.

[24] 'Hypocrite' was the common word for actors who pretended to be someone else when on stage.

[25] *The Ragamuffin Gospel,* page 136.

[26] *Life Together* (San Francisco: Harper and Row, 1954).

[27] *The Message.* (Colorado Springs, USA: NAVPRESS, 1995).

Chapter Six

The Heart of the Matter

It's all about Jesus

'To him who by means of his power working in us is able to do so much more than we can ever ask for, or even think of: to God be the glory in the church and in Christ Jesus for all time, for ever and ever! Amen.'

Some time ago in a certain small town, there lived a very wealthy, kind and generous gentleman (we shall call him 'Mr G' for 'generous'). Mr G was known and loved by everyone for the many things he did and paid for to make the town a beautiful and safe place in which to live. The residents owed so many things to him – the children's play area in the park, the new wing of the hospital, the science laboratory in the school, the day centre for the elderly, to mention a few – that they decided to express their appreciation by throwing a party for the entire town. Streets and buildings were decorated; special food was prepared; entertainers were hired; and, much to his astonishment, the kind Mr G was invited as guest of honour.

The party was an outstanding success. Everyone went home tired but happy. Saying 'thank you' in this way made people feel even better than they had expected. As for Mr G, he thought he must be the happiest man in the world. The party was so successful that the following year it was repeated, except that it was better than the year before. Once again

Mr G was the centre of attention, and once again the event had the effect of drawing people together and making them feel proud of their community. Gradually, without anyone's intending it, the celebrations in Mr G's honour became an annual event. Year after year the special day was repeated, and year after year the event was bigger and better than the one before.

And then one year, the unthinkable happened. The festivities were almost finished; the food was all gone and it was nearly time for the appreciation speeches, when one of the organizers casually inquired where the now elderly Mr G was. No one, it turned out, had seen him. And that's hardly surprising, because Mr G was at home, dozing in his fireside chair, quite unaware of what was going on. You can hardly blame him. After all, each year the party plans were kept a secret till the last moment, and this year was no exception, apart from the fact that, when the 'last moment' came, they had completely forgotten to invite him! So it was that the people celebrated, but the reason for the celebrations was missing.

Such things should never happen, but sometimes they do, even to the best of us. And in case you are thinking that you would never be guilty of such an oversight, the picture of the most serious oversight of all is described in Scripture, especially for you and me – this generation. The Speaker is none other than Jesus, and He is calling to Christians who claim to be part of His last-day church: *"'Listen! I stand at the door and knock; if anyone hears my voice and opens the door, I will come into his house and eat with him, and he will eat with me."'*[2]

Amazing, isn't it? Jesus is actually standing outside His own front door. It's His own front door because, in scriptural terms, He is married to the person on the inside, whether you think of that person as an individual Christian or the church as a whole. Addressed as it is to the church in Laodicea, this message is for those who once had, or think they have, a special relationship with Him. But something is horribly wrong. Though not yet divorced, husband (Christ) and the wife (church or Christian) are living separate lives, and Jesus comes to plead

for reconciliation. Not that He is the cause of the problem – it is the wife's love that has become lukewarm. So Jesus knocks on the door of her heart. He could force His way in if He wanted to, but He is not that kind of person. This door has to be opened from the inside.

What is really happening here? Illogical it may be, but here is a Christian who lives life without Christ. Here is a church which sings, and prays, and listens to sermons – and leaves God on the outside. Apart from the fact that the entrance is overgrown with weeds, because it is so long since the door was opened, the Christian looks like a Christian and the church looks like a church. There's a party going on inside; but the One for whom the party was planned is missing. This is the secular Christian and the secular church. They believe God exists, and every week they celebrate the life, death and resurrection of Jesus. But the living presence of Jesus is forgotten; so the celebrations of Christian lifestyle and worship are a formality.

Remember, it could be you and me and our present church described in the picture. We can be 'living our Christian lives', doing what we have always done week after week, Sabbath after Sabbath, but be totally out of touch with Jesus and the real world He has called us to serve. The worst thing of all is, we may not even realize there's a problem.

Everything may feel OK. As we look at ourselves in the mirror we may feel justified in thinking, 'Not bad. Not brilliant either, but no worse than Pastor Smith, that's for sure.' Or the church board may do the annual review of membership, church building and finances, and feel quite pleased with the way things are. With twenty baptisms from the evangelistic programme, the successful stewardship seminar, the launch of the Saturday night soup run and the installation of the new sound system, to all appearances the church is *'rich and well off'*[3] and in need of nothing, except, of course, more of what it's already got.

Which may not be a lot in the Lord's eyes. He looks at us, as He looks at His church, and He may see only spiritual poverty, nakedness and blindness.[4] Why? Because basically, as the Lord once told the prophet Samuel, *'"I do not judge as man judges. Man looks at the outward appearance, but **I look at the heart."**'*[5] Even as Christians we find it easier to measure our Christianity by externals such as knowledge of Scripture, the performance of the preacher and the choir, church membership, money in the bank, buildings, furnishings, events, programmes, rules, and standards, while Jesus measures it by one thing only: the quality of our relationships – our relationships with one another, but especially our relationship with Him.

There must be all sorts of reasons why we see things so differently from the way God sees them. Perhaps one of them is that the picture of God which the Bible paints for us seems just too good to be true. That portrait of unlimited grace, unconditional forgiveness and acceptance, extravagant love, and fatherly tenderness just doesn't compare with the pre-conceived ideas we have of God. Perhaps, as C. S. Lewis suggests, it's easier for people to think of God as being more like themselves: cantankerous, vindictive, forgetful, determined to keep us in our place. But as he points out: 'If you do not believe that the Absolute passionately wants to be our Friend and our Lover, then by all means reject such a seemingly absurd notion . . . (But) you can't be a Christian unless you believe that.'[6]

So that's the bottom line. Christianity is *'not primarily a moral code but a grace-laden mystery; it is not essentially a philosophy of love but a love affair; it is not keeping the rules with clenched fists but receiving a gift with open hands.'*[7] And, wonder of wonders, that gift is Jesus.

To state the obvious, Christianity is about Christ. He is the heart of the matter. If He is not at the centre of everything, the church is a sham, an empty shell. Unless we worship with a conscious sense of His presence in our midst, we do not really worship. Unless each one of our twenty-seven fundamental doctrines serves to foster our relationship with Him, it has no meaning. And unless those to whom we minister, Christians and non-Christians, feel the divine-human touch of Jesus on their lives, we are wasting our time 'doing the Lord's work'. My future church must be Christ-centred above everything else. We should, therefore, look a little closer and understand what this could mean in practical terms. For convenience, we consider Jesus, the Heart of things, under four headings:

The Heart of Community
The Heart of Worship
The Heart of Our Message
The Heart of Evangelism

The Heart of Community

My church may be large or it may be small. It may own its own church building or it may meet in a rented room over a Chinese take-away. The pastor may be old or young, experienced or inexperienced, a dynamic preacher or an informa-

tive teacher. There may be many talents or few; worship may be contemporary or traditional. But none of these things is going to make my future church essentially better or worse than another. In fact, it's possible to have the best in church facilities and activities and still not have a real

church. Remember, the church is neither a building nor an organization, but people, with Jesus in the centre. Essentially, the church is a unique, divine-human community.

'"For where two or three come together in my name, I am there with them."' [8]

'The church, you see, is not peripheral to the world; the world is peripheral to the church. The church is Christ's body, in which he speaks and acts, by which he fills everything with his presence.' [9]

A wonderful promise, a wonderful truth. But you can't have one without the other. You can, therefore, meet with other baptized church members in a beautiful church building to sing hymns or study the Bible, and not experience 'church'. On the other hand, you can invite a non-Christian friend to go ten-pin bowling with you so that you can introduce him to some other Christian friends, and that non-Christian friend can catch a glimpse of what the true church is like and how it works. How come? Because when Christians meet in His name – wherever that happens to be – Jesus is not just with them in the sense that they are three and His presence makes four. He is with them in the sense that He lives within them and among them, and He makes Himself known to them and through them because they are His body.

His life, not ours

Because the church is, first of all, the people of God and not buildings or organizations, I would suggest that the definition of the life of an authentic Christian would also define the life of an authentic Christian congregation. In my view, it is hard to improve on this: *'I have been put to death with Christ on his cross, so that it is no longer I who live, but it is Christ who lives in me. This life that I live now, I live by faith in the Son of God, who loved me and gave his life for me.'*[10]

You can probably think of all kinds of implications for these words if you apply them to your church. As I apply them to my future church, I have to ask a question or two:

- Is my church willing to be *'crucified with Christ'*, and be more concerned with His life than its own? Is it willing to risk its own reputation for His sake, or is its own survival more important?

- Are we as gracious towards the Mary Magdalenes in our fellowship as Jesus was towards her?

- Is my church more interested in making Christians than Seventh-day Adventists? Which is higher on our agenda – discipleship or church membership?

- As the Head of the body, is there a sense that Jesus is personally involved in the decision-making process of the church? Is it governed rigidly by rules and regulations, or are decisions sometimes taken as He communicates directly through the spiritual gifts of its members?

Christ-centred unity

It seems to me that more is being said and written these days about unity than ever before, which suggests we are still searching for it. We all want it, but how can we achieve it? Since the world became a global village, in many ways people are closer to one another than they've ever been, but in other ways they're farther apart. The nearer that market forces move us towards a single global culture, the more we struggle to preserve our cultural differences. Unfortunately, to some extent it's the same in the church. Barriers of mistrust still divide one group from another. The wall of partition which Jesus came to break down still appears to be standing firm in some places. Surely, it's time for it to go once and for all!

I believe my future church is going to be a place where unity is no longer a problem, because the source and centre of unity will have shifted from where it tends to be at the moment. Let's face it: the centre of Christian unity was never intended to be a common life-style, a single form of worship, or even agreement about every detail of our beliefs, but a Person – the person of Jesus. Christ's prayer was not simply *"that they may all be one'"* but that they may *"'be in us.'"*[11] What does that mean, as far as the unity of the church is concerned?

As we saw in chapter four, there is wonderful personal freedom in being *'in Christ'*. As He explained in His first synagogue sermon,[12] He came to liberate us from all that prevents us from being the people we were created to be. Far from stifling individuality, the Christian message encourages it. The church is not supposed to be a gathering of religious clones or stereotypes, but a marvellous display of human variety. It would be a travesty, therefore, if Christians were expected to lose their personal identity in order to achieve unity together. If liberty is God's gift to us, which it is, we should celebrate that liberty and all it means. And that means celebrating our differences, not hiding or denying them.

The question is, how can we be united and different at the same time? The answer has to be, the same way it happens in the rest of God's creation. The church is like a body;[13] it performs its function well *because* it has many different parts, not in spite of it. The same goes for the entire ecosystem: it flourishes because of the variety within it, not in spite of it. Apparently, the entire universe operates this way.

One of the glories of the solar system of which we are a part is just how different the other eight planets are to our own planet Earth. Jupiter is much larger; Saturn has those beautiful rings around it; Pluto is far more distant from the sun. Each has its own unique orbit, which means that sometimes certain planets are much closer to one another than at other times. What holds it all together? Primarily, the Sun does. The Sun is at the centre of every individual but one different orbit. In addition to that, the gravity of each planet influences the orbit of every other planet, helping to keep each one on course rather than its being sent off course. The result is perfect balance, one celestial unity, thanks to the power of gravity.

As it is in the celestial world, so it can be in the spiritual world. Just as the solar system consists of the sun and nine very different planets moving in different orbits around it, so the church consists

of Jesus and the very different people who live very different lives *'in Him'*. And just as the gravity of the sun holds it all together in one solar system, so the love of the Son of God holds us all together in one Christian community – even when we're far apart! Unity is found in communion with Him.

This kind of unity in community is, I repeat, unique. Because it is *'in Christ'* it is driven not by selfish or idealogical motives, but by love. Scott Peck defines this love as *'the will to extend one's self for the purpose of nurturing one's own or another's spiritual growth'.*[14] In my opinion, this is one of the best definitions of God's love there is. It's about giving rather than grabbing. This was the love that motivated Jesus to become less than He was to help us become more than we are, and it must be the love that motivates us.

'Let your attitude to life be that of Christ Jesus himself. For he, who had always been God by nature, did not cling to his privileges as God's equal, but stripped himself of every advantage by consenting to be a slave by nature and being born a man. And, plainly seen as a human being, he humbled himself by living a life of utter obedience, to the point of death, and the death he died was the death of a common criminal. That is why God has now lifted him to the hights, and has given him the name beyond all names . . . .'[15]

United – but different. That's how we can be in Christ. We can be mature enough as Christians, secure enough in our relationship with Christ, that we will not be fazed by those who think differently from ourselves and operate in a different church orbit. I want my future church to encourage individuality among its members. And I wish the same for *our* future church. I look forward to the day when congregations around the country and around the world differ much more than they do now. Each one will remain unquestionably Seventh-day Adventist; each one will be unquestionably part of the world-wide Adventist community. But each one will be different, unique, as it encourages the development of the unique people in its membership, and as it responds to the unique neighbourhood it serves. Different churches for different people. But that won't be a problem. Because the heart of this community is Christ.

The Heart of Worship

If Jesus is to be the Heart of our community, so He must be the Heart of worship. But what does that mean? Just as *'praying without ceasing'* means more than literally praying all day, so *'Christ-centred worship'* means more than just talking about Him during the worship service. It is interesting to note that nowhere in the New Testament are the two Greek words for *'worship'* used to describe a period of time or a gathering of people associated with acts of worship. *'Acceptable worship'* has far more to do with a seven-day offering of our lives to Him in service.[16] Sabbath worship is acceptable only as it is part of a life of worship. It's all about recognizing and experiencing Christ's presence from beginning to end of those periods set apart for this purpose.

Take a typical Sabbath morning programme. Which do you consider to be the more worshipful, Sabbath school or divine service? And within the 'divine' or 'worship' service, which of the following regular items would you consider to be the most worshipful, and which the least?

- Song service
- Announcements
- Hymns
- Welcome
- Scripture readings

- Prayer
- Lesson study
- Children's story
- Special music items
- Sermon
- Benediction

For most people, just as the divine service would probably be considered more worshipful than the Sabbath school, so the prayer would probably be considered more worshipful than the children's story. As for the announcements, we could do without them altogether, but there would be no point in going to church if there was no sermon. Right? Not necessarily.

Have you ever listened to a Christ-less sermon? *'At least once',* did you say? Well, have you ever shed a tear during the announcement period? Yes? I hope you see the point. Every item can be an important part of worship, *if* it is Christ-centred. If going to church is a weekly obligation, a religious ritual to go through from opening hymn to benediction, nothing is going to happen. But if the living presence of Jesus is anticipated and recognized from beginning to end, the whole of our Sabbath morning together can be a worshipful response to that Presence – including the break between the services! How can it be otherwise?

So there are probably just two requirements for a Christ-centred worship experience:

The right kind of attitude – thinking right.

The right kind of activity – doing things right.

However excellent and Christ-centred the item, if members come with the wrong attitude or expectations, they will not have a true worship experience. On the other hand, if worshippers come in the right frame of mind but the service itself leaves much to be desired, the worship experience will be spoiled. So let's look at these two areas in a bit more detail.

Thinking right

You know from experience that real worship doesn't just happen the way the light comes on at the flick of a switch. In order to experience the presence of Christ, you have to be in the right frame of mind. I'm not referring here to the importance of getting to church on time or avoiding arguments in the car along the way, although both are desirable if not always achievable. I'm talking more along the lines of thinking right about God and thinking right about ourselves. In other words, do we have something to worship God for?

In chapter four we considered what it means to 'live the truth'. There can be no real worship if we do not constantly acknowledge the truth about ourselves, and the amazing truth about the God who knows the way we are and loves and accepts us just the same. And since the church is people, not buildings, there can be no true worship unless we accept the fact that *'the Gospel of grace is an irresistible call to love (other people) the same way.'*[17] Worship is an acknowledgement and celebration of relationships, not achievements.

As far as Sabbath worship is concerned, we would gain far more from the experience if we were involved with Jesus during the week in that which is most important to Him – bringing people to Himself, and bringing people together. As we see Him at work in people's lives, including our own, we won't have to wait till Sabbath to get excited about the Christ we serve.

In this connection, it's worth mentioning that more and more Adventists are discovering that Sabbath worship is better than ever since they became involved with a small-group meeting midweek. On the one hand, small groups offer a unique setting for meeting the living Christ through fellowship and worship, and that experience can *'spill over'* into the corporate worship setting on Sabbath. On the other hand, a well-organized small-group ministry can take some of the pressure off the Sabbath. And that brings us to the second requirement of a Christ-centred worship experience:

Doing right

One of the reasons why 'Sabbath worship' is not always all it could be is that we try to pack too many things into it. Possibly because it's the only time when the whole church family is together, we feel we must use it to accomplish everything – preaching, teaching, fellowshipping, promoting, informing, organizing, discussing, collecting, distributing, witnessing, serving, and a whole lot more. And rather than enjoy the Sabbath's peace and rest, we end up frustrated, because we've not been able to do anything particularly well, and worn out, because we've tried to do more on the Sabbath than it was designed for.

The role of small-group ministry in the church is discussed more fully elsewhere in this book, but suffice it to say here that many things we try to do on Sabbath could be done much more effectively in small groups during the week, and the Sabbath itself could be what it was intended to be – a Christ-centred day of celebration and renewal.

No distractions

The key to Christ-centred worship is surely to focus and stay focused on His presence and the experience and practice of His grace. Many things can help or hinder this experience, including:

- **The subject:** It may be stating the obvious, but every worship service should be an opportunity for a visitor to understand the Gospel and learn the truth about God, and for Christians to deepen their acquaintance with Him. Those who prefer the heat of the 'fire and brimstone' approach should take a leaf out of the sermon notebook of the master Preacher . . .

   'Christ's favourite theme was the paternal character and abundant love of God. This knowledge of God was Christ's own gift to men, and this gift He has committed to His people to be communicated by them to the world.'[18]

- **Organization and 'flow':** Worshipful services are usually planned well in advance, so that every item 'flows' within a single Christ-centred theme. A worship committee can be a great help in achieving this.

- **Use of worship music:** Many hymns are not worship hymns at all, but a way of teaching doctrine. There is a place for these, but the best worship hymns are those that focus on the person and acts of God, especially those which are sung to Him rather than about Him. The song service that is used in some churches simply to fill the time between services or to stop people talking is not likely to be worshipful. It may also make a  nonsense of the 'opening hymn' that often follows it. Far better to provide an actual break between services, then begin the worship service itself with a time of singing which takes the place of an opening hymn.

- **Relevance:** Unless Bible translation, style of music, sermon topic, prayer language, etc. are meaningful, and unless visitors are 'guided' through the service from the platform so that they can understand what is happening, participation in worship will be minimal.

 ✾ **Reverence:** Reverence is not quietness but a natural response to an awareness of God's greatness and goodness. Joyful celebration is just as appropriate in His presence as prayerful penitence. Constant calls from the pulpit for reverence may have the opposite effect to the one intended on the spirit of worship.

 ✾ **Platform party:** Is it really necessary to have those taking part on display throughout the service? Probably they, as well as the congregation, could better concentrate on worship if they were seated on the front row when not playing their part.

If all this sounds critical, I suppose it is, but it's meant to be constructive, not destructive. It's a plea that we get serious about worship – in the right sense of the word. We need to stop 'playing' church, and learn to *be* the church at worship.

The Heart of the Message

What, exactly, do Seventh-day Adventists believe? What is our special contribution to the Christian church supposed to be? What are the three angels' messages actually all about? Other writers are better able to answer those questions, and this  book is supposed to encourage you to envision your future church and then go for it, rather than to become sidelined with theological detail. But there is room here for one crucial observation:

'The sacrifice of Christ as an atonement for sin is the great

truth around which all other truths cluster. In order to be rightly understood and appreciated, every truth in the Word of God, from Genesis to Revelation, must be studied in the light that streams from the cross of Calvary.[19]

Not so long ago, when conducting a Bible study series or a baptismal class, I used to deal with salvation in Christ as a topic, along with the state of the dead, the millennium, the Sabbath and all the others. There was one study on justification, another on sanctification, and that was about the only time that Christ was the centre of the message. To be sure, I tried to include something of what Jesus said in all the other studies, although on some subjects I noticed He said very little. But I can't honestly say the whole message – the Adventist message as I understood and presented it – was truly Christ-centred.

Now I am beginning to see things more clearly, and I like what I see. The Advent message is special because Jesus is the Heart of it in a unique kind of way. That includes the difficult bits of the book of Revelation, although you may agree that we still have some work to do in that area. My future church can make no claim that it is special, apart from the message it has to share; and if Jesus is not the heart and soul of it then we had better not share it! We cannot say that our church is better than other churches, and we must never say that those who belong to other churches know Him less well than we do. It's just that the message God has entrusted us with has a unique potential for glorifying Jesus, and if we don't see that clearly now, one day we shall.

Good news, not bad

Christians and their message have not always had the most positive press, so it's not surprising if Adventists are given a hard time. If Christians generally are knows as kill-joys, Adventists are known (if they are known at all) for all the things we don't do, can't do, or shouldn't do but do anyway, and there are obviously reasons for that. But if we are really serious about who we are and what our mission is, somehow the truth needs to come out. We need to understand it, experience it, and share it with others, that our message – all of it – is *Good News,* not bad.

Maybe it's because God knew that we would have an uphill road to climb in getting the message across, that He made sure that John saw those three messengers of Revelation as bearers of *'an eternal message of Good News'* for everyone on Earth. That's not how it is perceived, but that's how it needs to be understood. What can be done to shift from negative mode to positive mode? The answer has to be found in Jesus.

As you are probably aware, Ellen White was often asked if the message of justification by faith in Christ had anything to do with the third angel's message of Revelation chapter fourteen, and her answer was always the same: *'It is the third angel's message in verity.'*[20] In modern parlance, that means *'Yes, definitely! God's last message for people is the same as it has always been: it's all about Jesus.'* The person of Jesus, His love for us, and what He has done and is doing for us is the treasure we have to share with one another and our non-Christian friends. We have nothing else worthwhile to offer. My future church must learn how to share it well, and, when it does, the message may well prove irresistible!

Christ-Centred Sabbaths

The most obvious thing about Adventists is the fact that we keep Sabbath on Saturday. Apart from the way we live our lives during the week, the fact is that our Sabbath-keeping has more potential for creating a positive or negative image in people's minds of the God we serve, than any other of our beliefs. So in my future church, the centre of every Sabbath must be Jesus. Do we have some growing to do in this area?

Ask a dozen Adventists why they keep the Sabbath and why others should do the same, and you may well get one of these answers:

- Because the Bible says so.
- It's a memorial of creation.
- It's a duty – it's in the Ten Commandments.
- It's a test of our loyalty to God.
- Because Sunday is 'the mark of the beast'.

When church members have been asked in surveys I have conducted over the years whether they see Sabbath-keeping as an obligation or not, the majority have always said, 'Yes'. We all know that there's more to it than that, but that's the bottom line – it's an obligation, and therefore not always the joyful, liberating, Christ-centred experience it's meant to be. And that's the impression our non-Adventist friends have picked up from us, so some of them call us legalists.

Since the Sabbath is so central to our message, and because the way we keep Sabbath is a tangible way of measuring what the good news of Jesus means to us, we should look more closely at how Jesus understood and kept it. (Having completed this exercise with this doctrine, it would be worth doing the same with the rest of what we believe, just to make sure He really is the heart of things.)

Day of Celebration

It certainly seems as though the Sabbath was a day of celebration for Jesus. From His first Sabbath sermon to His last Sabbath miracle, the consistent message was, *'There's more*

good news than bad. God is alive, and He is here to help!',
and the common people loved Him for it. Sadly, not all were
happy with that message, because it didn't match their
traditional, somewhat masochistic view of the Sabbath.
Consequently, Jesus faced more confrontation and controversy on the Sabbath and about the Sabbath than at any other
time or about any other subject, apart from the subject of who
He claimed to be.

Sabbath was not usually a happy event for ordinary people
in Christ's day. Again and again we read that people were
angry, upset, afraid, and miserable on the Sabbath. They
lived in constant fear that they could be breaking one of a
thousand Sabbath rules without realizing it. Writing as a
physician, Luke records that many patients with medical
problems of one sort or another, waited till after sunset on
Sabbath before they came to Jesus. Why? Because they were
afraid of what might happen to them if they went to Jesus for
healing during the Sabbath.

And so the Sabbaths came and went. God was among His
people; this extraordinary Jesus walked among ordinary men
and women; but those Sabbaths were days of sadness instead
of joy, darkness instead of light, loneliness instead of love,
confrontation instead of celebration. What a shame! Because
that's not how it was meant to be. And Jesus was determined
to put the record straight.

He didn't have to do what He did on the Sabbath. He did
not enjoy conflict, and He could have avoided it. The fact is
that He seemed to go out of His way to do the things that
caused the conflict, and in the process healed and helped
twice as many people on Sabbath as on any other day.
Obviously, He was making a statement, and that statement
was that the Sabbath is a gift. It never was intended to be an
obligation.

Think what it must have been like to be with Jesus on Sabbath. Imagine the scenes in the following stories, and grasp the principles that made the Sabbath so special for Him:

Principle: The Sabbath was made for our good (Mark 2:23-28).

The Scene: Jesus and His disciples are walking through a cornfield, possibly on their way to worship. The disciples have probably missed breakfast and are hungry; so begin to eat the corn. Pharisees accuse them of Sabbath breaking. Jesus sees no conflict between this kind of activity and keeping Sabbath.

Application: The Sabbath was designed to meet our needs. We were not designed to fit into the Sabbath. One of the blessings of the Sabbath is that, whenever possible, we would do well to prepare for the Sabbath in advance so we can be free to focus on the more important things in life, especially the building of relationships with God and other people. Sabbath is more about the Creator and His family than simply 'creation'.

Principle: Jesus is Lord of the Sabbath.

The Scene: As above. Religious leaders in conflict with Jesus over the interpretation of the law concerning the Sabbath. He claims to be the final authority on such matters.

Application: The heart of the Sabbath is Jesus, not the food on your table, or other rules or regulations for that matter. His word and His example are sufficient for us, even in the face of Old Testament directives which may appear to require a more legalistic approach to Sabbath keeping.[21]

Principle: Doing good is consistent with keeping Sabbath (Matthew 12:9-14; Mark 3:5)

The Scene: Jesus heals a paralyzed man 'in church' on Sabbath, and the same religious leaders who met Jesus in the cornfield challenge Him again. They see a conflict between helping a fellow man and keeping the Sabbath. Jesus sees harmony between the two.

Application: Keeping the law (the 'law that sets people free'[22]) consists of doing good, not only of refraining from doing evil. In a positive sense, the arrival of the Sabbath can mean an increase in our Christian 'work load' as it did for Jesus, but it is in this way particularly that the Sabbath can brings its blessings. Anything that enhances our appreciation for life, or enables us to share more fully in the life of God; anything that helps us share one another's lives more deeply; anything that renews life, restores life, or improves life, is a part of God's purpose for the Sabbath. It's a day for the celebration of *life!*

Principle: Sabbath is a day of liberation (Luke 13:10-17)

The Scene: In a crowded synagogue Jesus notices a lady who has been unable to stand upright for eighteen years because of a malady inflicted by Satan. Jesus heals her *because it's the Sabbath,* not in spite of it, as if the Sabbath is the best day of the week to do this kind of thing. The synagogue official is outraged, but the crowd celebrates.

Application: The Sabbath is more than a celebration of creation – it's a celebration of *re*creation. Blessed and sanctified by Christ above the others, the Sabbath is the most appropriate day of all for men and women to receive deliverance from whatever binds them.[23]

It's well worthwhile reading all the stories of Christ's

Sabbath ministry, just to get the complete picture of how He understood its meaning and purpose. It really seems that His entire mission, God's gift of salvation, and the weekly Sabbath, were inseparably linked together in a unique way.

The Adventist Advantage

Christ's relation to the Sabbath implies that those who understand and observe it with Him as its focus possess a unique advantage over other Christians who do not understand its message. Wherever He went, people rejoiced as they saw both the Sabbath in the light of His grace, and His grace in the light of the Sabbath. And nothing has changed. On this day, more than the others:

- Jesus meets with His people in mercy and power to heal and renew. We should be able to witness His healing, liberating presence among us perhaps more than we do.
- The re-creative energy that it brings is the very thing a tired and stressed-out generation needs. The Sabbath was made for them, too!
- There is a unique opportunity to experience and understand the meaning of salvation. While it is our privilege to live within the grace of God every day, the Sabbath is a day when His grace can come with extra richness into special focus. For this reason alone, maybe we should make our Sabbath services more evangelistic, more seeker-sensitive, than we have done.

Probably we could list other advantages as well. The point is that my future church may need to be a bit more up-front about the Sabbath, and a bit less apologetic than yesterday's church has been.[24]

We're not talking about sharing an obligation here, but an opportunity. The Sabbath is first of all a privilege, not a duty. It's not another test or another problem, but a great advantage in the journey of life. That should be fairly obvious, of course, if Jesus is not just the Heart of the Sabbath, but the Heart of the entire message.

The Heart of Evangelism

If Jesus is the Heart of the matter – our community, our worship, and our message – who knows what He will accomplish through His church? He was the Heart of the matter once before, and the result was Pentecost. Should we expect anything less? I don't think so. The best days for evangelism are still future, and we had better be ready for them! The Jesus of the Gospels – whom some suggest has to be the best-kept secret of Christianity – has to be the Heart of evangelism, too. For the purpose of this chapter, that means two things: leading people to Jesus, and following His method.

Leading people to Jesus. Evangelism – proclaiming the Good News – has to do with leading people to faith in Christ rather than to acceptance of a belief system or membership of the church. Stuart Murray has something interesting to say on this:

'We live in a society which is heartily sick of Christianity but which has yet to encounter Jesus. And it may be the story of Jesus, rather than doctrinal beliefs about Jesus, that will prove to be our most potent evangelistic resource. Walter Wink suggests: "In the spiritual renaissance that I believe is coming to birth, it will not be the message of Paul that this time galvanises hearts, as in the Reformation and the Wesleyan revival, but the human figure of Jesus."'[25]

Former generations of Adventists might have seen it as their *primary* mission to call Christians out of other churches and into their own, but it surely can no longer be ours. In many parts of the Western World, less than ten per cent of the population attends a Christian church. Are we really supposed to ignore the other ninety per cent, or is it the responsibility of the other churches to do the real evangelism?

The truth is, of course, that whatever evangelism, we do simply isn't evangelism if Christ is not at the beginning of it, the heart of it, and the end of it. Let's not fool ourselves: large crowds may attend our meetings: many baptisms may result, and church membership may grow: but that in itself is not proof of effective evangelism. Our commission is to make disciples,[26] fully-devoted followers of Christ,[27] nothing more, nothing less. As He explained:

'As Moses lifted up the bronze snake on a pole in the desert, in the same way the Son of Man must be lifted up, so that everyone who believes in him may have eternal life.' And *'"When I am lifted up from the earth, I will draw everyone to me."'* And *'"I am the way, the truth, and the life; no one goes to the Father except by me."'*[28]

Follow His method. Apparently no other method will work. There is only one way, not many ways.

'Christ's method alone will give true success in reaching the people. The Saviour mingled with men as one who desired their good. He showed His sympathy for them, ministered to their needs, and won their confidence. Then he bade them, "Follow me."'[29]

This method is astonishing in its simplicity! So simple that we are likely to overlook it or dismiss it. Compared to the modern methods that churches and evangelists use, we would probably have said that it was crazy or unworkable if Christ Himself had not modelled it. But it's there for all to see in the gospels, and who would dare to suggest they know a better way! The following observations of my own are added, for what they may be worth:

- **It's about people, not proof texts.** Then, as now, it seems, the question ordinary people were asking was more likely to be *'does it work?'* than *'is it true?'* They were sick of the constant arguments among religious leaders over details that were irrelevant to their lives. Jesus' ministry was a breath of fresh air to them, because they knew He was more interested in their needs than in proving a point or winning an argument.

- **It's a way of life.** It's obvious from reading the gospels that evangelism was not one task among many for Jesus, but the overall purpose of His life. To Jesus, 'seeking the lost' was not a programme or an event with a beginning and an end, but a 365-days-a-year focus. Helping, healing, teaching, preaching, even eating – it was all evangelism to Jesus. He seized evangelistic opportunities as Providence created them, whether it was the sight of the lonely woman by Jacob's well, Nicodemus's night-time visit, or a hungry multitude.

  It follows that evangelism in my future church will not be one department among other departments, but the reason for everything we do. The church's entire programme must be evangelistically oriented. We will need not only effective ways of building relationships with new people and sharing Jesus with them, but a warm, safe and friendly atmosphere in church meetings, a culturally relevant worship style, and adequate opportunities for nurture, growth and gifts-based ministry, if we are to succeed in making, developing and multiplying disciples for Christ.

✦ **It's relaxed.** Was Jesus ever stressed? If He was, it didn't have a negative effect on His ministry. He clearly felt the weight of the huge responsibilities resting upon Him, but He remained serene except when faced with the scandal of the money changers. How did He handle the pressures of His life-work with such serenity? He handled it by understanding that His work was first of all His Father's work. I hope that I and the other members of my future church will learn to have the same unworried approach to evangelism that He had, and for the same reason. Jesus explained that *'"the Son can do nothing on his own; he does only what he sees his Father doing. What the Father does, the Son also does."'*[30]

In the past we have probably been guilty of trying to do what it was never our job to do. With the help of a committee, we've decided where, when and how we will do our evangelism, and then asked God to bless our efforts. Jesus took the opposite approach, trying first to see where the Father was already working, and then joining in with Him. That way He was assured of His blessing. Of course, God guides committees, too, especially when they are open to His leading. But I sense my future church has some growing to do in this area.

✦ **It's focused.** The most important part of Christ's evangelistic strategy was the training of the few in order to reach the many. As we have observed, as far as His own evangelism was concerned, He never went out to conduct a 'crusade'. He simply met people where they were, followed as His Father led Him, and made the best use of opportunities as they came to Him, whether His audience was a crowd or a single individual. At the end of His life, there wasn't much to show for His labours. It was what He

111

gave His disciples that made the difference in the long term.

'Robert Coleman describes Jesus' training of the few to reach the many as "the genius of His strategy". He writes: "Though He did what He could to help the multitudes, He had to devote Himself primarily to a few men, rather than the masses, in order that the masses could at last be saved."'[31]

As Coleman goes on to say, we have to decide where we want our ministry to count – in the momentary applause of popular recognition or in the reproduction of our lives in a few chosen people who will carry on our work after we have gone.[32] Again and again we have been counselled as a church that the real potential for evangelism lies not with a few skilled evangelists, but with the mobilization of the membership as a whole. We will discuss how this might happen in chapter seven.

➤ **It's visionary.** Another reason why Jesus was so unstressed about His work and why He took so much time with the twelve disciples was that He saw beyond the present to the future. He saw not only what was, but what would be. When His disciples met Him after His conversation with the Samaritan woman at the well, He invited them to take a second look around them and try to see the future as He saw it, with large numbers of people coming to faith in Him. Similarly, when He sent out the seventy disciples two-by-two to prepare the way for His future visits, he envisioned a large harvest.[33]

Christ's method of evangelism was simple – and, in the

long term, it was incredibly successful. If we adopt His method, that success story may be repeated, even exceeded, in our day. True, those who have never heard the name of Jesus are more numerous than ever. But so is the number of Christians. Just one more universal, Pentecostal push, and it could all be over. Can you begin to imagine the celebration, the jubilation, in heaven when the work is done and the party begins? I can't – but I do want my future church to be a part of it.

And it will be, if Jesus is the Heart of the Matter.

Ephesians 3:20, 21.

The words of Revelation 3:20 are addressed to the church at Laodicea (see verse 14).

Rev. 3:17a.

Verse 17b.

1 Samuel 16:7.

C. S. Lewis, *The Problem of Pain* (New York: MacMillan), pages 49, 50.

Brennan Manning, page 214.

Matthew 18:20.

Ephesians 1:22b, 23, *The Message*.

Galatians 2:20.

John 17:21.

Luke 4:18, 19.

1 Corinthians 12:12-29.

M. Scott Peck, *The Road Less Travelled* (London: Arrow Books, 1990), page 85.

Philippians 2:5-9, J. B. Phillips.

Romans 12:1.

Brennan Manning, page 213.

Ellen G. White, *Testimonies to the Church*, vol. 6, page 55.

Ellen G. White, *Evangelism*, page 190.

ibid, page 190.

Lyndon K. McDowell, in his article, 'The Neglected Dimension of Sabbath Rest,' *Ministry*, February 1998, makes the observation in his footnotes that 'there is no reference anywhere in Scripture to any period in history when Israel kept the Sabbath properly; rather, the contrary,' and cites Ezekiel 20:13, 21; Jeremiah 17:19-27; 2 Chronicles 36:20-22; Romans 9:30-10:3. We should keep this in mind when attempting to apply the prophets' rebukes and corrective messages to the contemporary situation, and remember that the example of Jesus as 'Lord of the Sabbath' is the only one we should follow.

[22] James 1:25; 2:12.

[23] See also Luke 4:16-21, and how Jesus taught that Isaiah's promise of deliverance (Isaiah 61:1, 2) was fulfilled from that same Sabbath day.

[24] Ellen White wrote that with the final outpouring of the Holy Spirit, we will preach the Sabbath *'more fully.'* See *Early Writings*, pages 33, 85.

[25] Stuart Murray, *Church Growth Digest,* Autumn 1999 Moggerhanger, Beds, UK: British Church Growth Association, Article: Contemporary Trends and Their Implications for the Church, page 10.

[26] Matthew 28:19.

[27] A widely-used definition of a Christian disciple, originated by Bill Hybels, senior pastor of the Willow Creek Community Church, Chicago.

[28] John 3:14, 15; 12:32; 14:6.

[29] Ellen G. White, *The Ministry of Healing*, page 143.

[30] John 5:19.

[31] Robert Coleman, *The Master Plan of Evangelism,* page 33, quoted in Philip G. Samaan, *Christ's Way of Making Disciples* (Hagerstown, MD: Review and Herald, 1999), page 72.

[32] ibid., page 37.

[33] John 4:35; Luke 10:1, 2.

More Spirit

A Spirit-led, Spirit-filled church

'I do crave a more "felt" presence of God in my church.'- Alden Thompson

pace probes sent to search for evidence of life on other planets look for one thing before anything else – water. Everybody understands that life, at least as we know it, cannot exist without water. And if that applies to physical life, it also applies to spiritual life. What Jesus offers each person who trusts Him is not a set of dry ideas but thirst-quenching water that *'"will become in him a spring which will provide him with life-giving water and give him eternal life."'* And if this is not enough, the promised supply is so abundant that it flows, not just in trickles, but in streams 'pouring out' of our hearts to refresh others as well as ourselves. What is this remarkable life-giving water? According to Jesus, it is the Holy Spirit, through whom He both fills and leads those who believe in Him, who make up His church on earth.

A Spirit-filled church

Clearly, the purpose and work of the Holy Spirit is so bound up with the purpose and work of Jesus that it is impossible to separate the One from the Other. All we need say for the purpose of this chapter is:

- No water – no physical life
- No Holy Spirit – no spiritual life

If my future church is to be genuinely Christ-centred, it must also be Spirit-filled. If my church really is to be 'the body of Christ', not just in theory but in fact, through which He continues to walk and talk with people as He once did, the Spirit of Christ must fill every part of it, influencing every attitude and every action. It's a profound idea, and no one puts it better than the apostle Paul in that famous prison letter to the Ephesians:

'I ask God from the wealth of his glory to give you power through his Spirit to be strong in your inner selves, and I pray that Christ will make his home in your hearts through faith. I pray that you may have your roots and foundation in love, so that you, with all God's people, may have the power to understand how broad and long, how high and deep, is Christ's love. Yes, may you come to know his love – although it can never be fully known – and so be completely filled with the very nature of God?' [3]

This has to be one of the most amazing prayers of the entire Bible. The idea that ordinary human beings, who are selfish and small-minded by nature, can experience a love in their hearts so great it is incomprehensible belongs in the realm of the miraculous. To suggest that mortal men and women, who forget what they did yesterday, get toothache, and live in houses made of brick or stone, can become a dwelling place for the Divine would be utterly ridiculous, if it were not so sublimely true. It's the glory of the Gospel – Christ lives in people by His Spirit so He can love other people through them. By this means the church becomes His body, an extension of the incarnation.

Surely, if Paul prayed this kind of prayer, we can, too, for ourselves, for one another and for our churches. Because one thing is certain: God is not in the business of withholding or making us wait for a gift so crucial to human survival. That would be like a father and mother deliberately starving their children to death. Jesus assures us that if human parents, imperfect as they are, know how to give their children the things they need, our Father in heaven is much more willing to give the Holy Spirit to those who ask Him.[4]

Clearly, we have some serious asking to do. Not that praying for the Holy Spirit is anything new, of course. The church has been praying for the filling of the Holy Spirit for years, and we thank God for what He has given and what He has done. But we want more, much more. Maybe we need to do more than ask. Maybe we need to be more ready to receive. Which leads us to the question: Is there anything my future church can do, or refrain from doing, to allow that living water to flow more freely? Or is it all in God's hands?

Well, I happen to believe in a second Pentecost, but I don't believe that means there are any limits to what God is able and willing to give us now. The Spirit came at Pentecost to continue the work that Christ began, and there is no suggestion anywhere that He has left us to manage on our own since that time. If God is waiting for anything, He is waiting for us. As in the parable, the river has never stopped flowing from the mountains: it's the dam that has got in the way. (The dam was built with the best of intentions, but the long-term result was the death of the city. The dam has to go!)

A barrier-busting mentality

One thing is certain about the remnant church described in the book of Revelation: it has a 'dam-busting' mentality. Every old barrier that has prevented the free flow of the Spirit

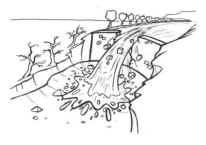

is removed, and no new one is built to take its place! Unhindered, the river of the Spirit flows to *'every race, tribe, language, and nation'* and Christ's work on Earth is finished. My church and your church can be part of that wonderful future, if we will learn from the past.

At first, the church was so closely connected to its divine Head through prayer and submission that the New Testament 'Acts of the Apostles' is often referred to as 'the acts of the Holy Spirit'. It had a simple system of organization and government so that everything could *'be done in a proper and orderly way,'*[5] and there is no doubt that the simplicity of the system itself was essential to the rapid growth which followed Pentecost.[6] But there was something else as well. It appears that the Holy Spirit was in direct charge of church affairs through laity as well as leaders who constantly asked for and submitted to His guidance.

But the control system of the church changed. Barriers which were deliberately or unwittingly built created a bottleneck of spiritual energy, and a once-dynamic, liberating movement of truth quickly became a giant barrier to progress. The true church of Jesus nearly died. How did it happen? What were the dams that did the damage? Bearing in mind that barriers are built for purposes of control, we could consider the following:

- **The power barrier.** The apostasy which led to the 'dark ages' of the church was caused not only by the substitution of falsehood for truth, but by the substitution of human control for the control of the Spirit. In fact, doctrinal error could never have spread through the church as rapidly as it did had it not been for the fact that the laity had been robbed of their priestly role.[7] It is not a coincidence that the first official step towards the change of the Sabbath, and the first official step towards the institutionalizing of the church were taken by the same person, Constantine. This Roman emperor built the first church buildings, and encouraged the unscriptural distinction between clergy and laity as a way of controlling the power of the growing church. The growth of a power-hungry, autocratic clergy created a barrier of control that to some extent remains in the Christian church even today.

Closer to home, in the early 1900s, the future of the Advent movement was threatened by a few well-meaning but power-hungry leaders who felt the need to control every aspect of the church's work. Only repeated prophetic messages of correction from the pen of Ellen White and the powerful presence of God in the 1901 General Conference session brought the organizational reforms which enabled the church to be more responsive to the leading of the Spirit.

Now, one hundred years later, some things have changed. Membership is much larger and more widespread. Methods of communication are faster and more efficient. Styles of leadership differ according to local culture. Different countries have widely different needs. Not surprisingly, multinational companies have had to make their management structures and styles much more flexible than before to accommodate these changes. Surely the most important company of all, the church, must build as much flexibility as possible into its management/decision-making process. Church manuals and protocol, departments and committees, pastors and presidents,

Conferences and Unions, all have their proper place. But now, more than at any other time, the free flow of the Spirit is all-important, so that every local congregation can respond to local needs and opportunities for ministry as rapidly as possible.

➤ **The fear barrier,** which can often be found behind the power barrier. The first-ever hand-over of power happened because our first parents were afraid of God's control. And the same is still true. Thanks to the excesses of legalism on the one hand and the extremes of the charismatic movement on the other, some of us are afraid of what might happen if the Spirit really did take control of our lives. Leaders, likewise, have their reasons to be afraid of what might happen if they allow others less experienced than themselves to take the reins of control.

But the fact is that where the Spirit is in control there's nothing to be afraid of. As we have already noted, His presence only renews our ability to love and be loved, and the truth into which He leads us brings true freedom, the liberty to live in harmony with God. As C. Mervyn Maxwell observed, Pentecost was all about obedience.

'The Day of Pentecost fell on the anniversary of the giving of the Ten Commandments on Mount Sinai . . .

' . . . it's high time that Seventh-day Adventists took "Pentecost" away from sensationalism and restored it to its proper significance as empowerment to obey.

' . . . So, on Pentecost, an anniversary of the giving of the Ten Commandments, the power fell, and immediately the disciples and their close associates obeyed. They went out into the streets and began to witness, to teach people to do what Jesus had said they should do.[8]

The tradition barrier. The fear barrier is built on the foundation of the unknown. Movement and change inevitably lead into uncharted waters. Most of us naturally feel more secure and comfortable with the old and familiar than with the new and strange. So even though the church is commissioned to preach a life-changing message about a revolutionary person called Jesus, it is resistant to change because the church is people. We would even rather work with 'the devil we know than the devil we don't'. And we forget that life is *about* change because life is about growth, and there can be no growth without change.

Probably the single most important reason why newly-planted churches are so full of energy and grow faster than established churches is that they don't have to struggle with the 'we've never done it that way before' attitude. As a church, let us recognize that there is such a thing as Adventist tradition. Some of it is good; some of it isn't. New wineskins for the new wine may be our greatest need.

The agenda barrier. Because certain methods worked well in the past, churches often approach their tasks with a fixed, pre-prepared agenda. Sometimes the agenda is very rigid, even closed. Board meetings and other committees need an agenda, of course, just as evangelism needs a method and church services need a programme. Naturally, we don't like it if our agendas are taken over by interruptions or surprises. I wonder if we have made it difficult for the Spirit to do His work because we have given our agenda priority over His.

The red-tape barrier. Some Adventist traditions began as methods or procedures which were appropriate at the time, but, because the church has grown and times have changed, what worked for us then may work against us now. Whatever the reasons, life for most people moves faster these days than it has ever done. Addressing the need for streamlining and efficiency in the local church, William Easum argues that *'the shorter the time lag between discovering a spiritual need and the implementation of a response in the form of a new ministry, the more effective the church will be in the twenty-first century.'*[9]

Since the efficiency of the local church is affected by the efficiency of the wider church, the same principle applies overall. The red tape of structures which duplicate effort and waste time may hinder or block completely the flow of spiritual ministry from source to goal.

The image barrier. As we have already observed, this is the age when it is important to look good. One of the spin-offs of our desire to 'be right' as a church is that we may have become more inward  looking than is good for us. One reason that is often given for why churches do not engage in evangelism or individuals do not share their faith is that they are 'not ready'. As if there will ever be a time when we are ready! Petersen's rendering of Romans 11:8 which describes the destructive self-interest of Old Testament Israel is worth including here:

'Fed up with their quarrelsome, self-centred ways, God blurred their eyes and dulled their ears, shut them in on themselves in a hall of mirrors, and they're there to this day.'

An inward-looking church is hardly compatible with an outward-reaching Saviour and His free-flowing Spirit!

A Spirit-led church

Imagine a church without these and other barriers to the working of God's Spirit! What might it look like? You may see your future barrier-free church differently from the way I see mine, but something tells me that all Spirit-led churches will have some characteristics in common. Here are a few:

The priority of prayer

Every Christian knows that prayer is important. As the 'breath of the soul' we can hardly do without it. But is the purpose of prayer simply to supply us with spiritual oxygen, or is there more to it than that? Obviously. Prayer is the means by which we give God thanks and make our requests known to Him. It is also the means by which we individually and corporately surrender our wills to Him, and come to know His will for us.

Does this sound familiar? It may be a church board meeting, a nominating committee or another important planning/ decision-making event, but it consists of three parts:

- We begin with a brief prayer for God's guidance.
- We then do whatever it is we have to do.
- We close with a brief prayer for God's blessing on our plans at the end.

The majority of time is usually taken sharing opinions and discussing options. In many situations that may well be the best way to proceed. In others, however, should we not seek to be more in tune with the mind of the Spirit by spending more time in prayer during the proceedings, not just at the beginning?

The church is His, not ours. Its mission is divine, not human. He has invited us to work with Him: it's hardly our place to invite Him to work with us. So it is more important for us to know His will than for Him to know ours, although He knows that anyway. It is more sensible to identify where He is already working and what He is already blessing, and join Him where He is, than for us to decide what we shall do and ask Him to bless it and join us where we are. We need to confess our almost total ignorance of what is best, and simply place ourselves at His disposal with a prayer like this:

'Holy Spirit, we don't really understand what the needs of this congregation are, and we don't know how to reach the people of this neighbourhood. Help us to see things as You see them. Lead us to those people, or those people to us, whom You want to minister to, and those You want as part of this church. We just want to be what You want us to be; we just want to do what You want us to do.'

Having prayed a prayer like that, we then need to listen. It just might be that God will answer! I confess that I'm not very good at listening in prayer, but I want to grow in this area. I think my future church will need to cultivate its listening ability in prayer.

Asking God to take the initiative in this way – and being open to His guidance – will take a lot more patience, perhaps a lot more spiritual maturity, than we are used to exercising. Adventists, probably more than most Christians, would rather be doing something than waiting for something to happen; following instead of leading does not fit our 'coming soon' message too well. But interesting things happen when Christians 'allow' God to be God. People walk into churches on Sabbath morning when no one has invited them. Church members begin to feel the excitement of seeing Him at work in their lives. And the way is open for big things to happen again. Remember, Pentecost was God's initiative.

Contagious enthusiasm

There is something very wonderful about the life Jesus offers to share with us, but all too often – usually a year or two after their conversion – Christians get bogged down with the details and lose sight of the big picture. True, the Christian life is not easy: no one ever said it would be. But once the details are put in their proper place and we focus once again on Jesus, the Heart of the message, our life in the Spirit can never be uninteresting or dull. *'Where the Spirit of the Lord is present, there is freedom'*[10] to enjoy, among other things, the *'life in all its fullness'* which Jesus came specifically to give us[11]. And that is hardly something to be half-hearted about!

Whether called by God to warn, reprove, or deliver good news, the Bible writers did what they did with passion and conviction. I get the impression that one of the things that drew people to Jesus, especially young people and children, was His love of life, His enthusiasm for His mission. And it wasn't an artificial, stiff-upper-lip enthusiasm, either. That's how He was. The God we serve is not remote, mechanical, unfeeling. He is *passionate* about us. It's not surprising, then, if one of the unlisted fruits of the Spirit is contagious enthusiasm for our faith.

One of the questions Christian Schwartz asked in his world-wide survey to establish the common denominators of growing churches was, *'Are the Christians in this church "on fire"? Do they live committed lives, and practise their faith with joy and enthusiasm?'* Responses from over one thousand growing, stagnant and declining churches of all kinds clearly showed that *'pure doctrine alone, as countless examples illustrate, does not induce growth. A church, regardless of how orthodox its dogma and view of Scripture, can hardly expect to experience growth, as long as its members do not learn to live their faith with contagious enthusiasm and to share this faith with others.'*[12]

Heartfelt worship

As Jesus once said, ' *"It's not **where** we worship that counts, but **how** we worship – is our worship spiritual and real? For God is Spirit, and we must have his help to worship as we should. The Father wants this kind of worship from us."* '[13]

Heartfelt worship is difficult to describe, but you know when it is happening. It is not measured by the loudness of the singing or by the presence or absence of repeated 'Amens' from the congregation. It is the natural and spontaneous response of people who sense they are in the active presence of a wonderful God. No one has expressed the experience better than William Temple:

'Worship is the submission of all our nature to God. It is the quickening of the conscience by His holiness; the nourishment of the mind with His truth; the purifying of the imagination by His beauty; the opening of the heart to His love; the surrender of will to His purpose; and all these gathered up in adoration, the most selfless emotion of which our nature is capable, and therefore the chief remedy for that self-centredness which is original sin and the source of all actual sin.'[14]

We cannot make this kind of heartfelt worship happen, but we can help to create an atmosphere which is conducive to it. Whether in the formal setting of the church building on Sabbath or the informal setting of a church member's home

during the week, some things can contribute towards a heart-felt worship-experience, including:
- pleasant décor,
- appropriate and well-presented worship music,
- well-planned and co-ordinated programmes,
- punctuality in starting worship services,
- an absolute minimum of non-worship items,
- worshipful themes for meditation.

Even more important than these considerations, however, is our attitude to our fellow worshippers.

To illustrate: in one particular church I attended some years ago, the first elder (who was also the organist) seemed to equate reverence with silence and sadness. The way he glared at teenagers who attempted to communicate with one another during Sabbath services, even by a whisper, was so aggressive that if looks  could kill they would never have survived. Smiling while he was speaking was an even worse offence. I think the poor man thought people who smiled were making fun of him. Two teenage sisters with particularly sunny natures were counselled so often about the need to be more serious in church that it's amazing they continued coming!

It's true that the Spirit's presence among us may sometimes lead to a sense of sorrow or solemnity, and unfortunately some people are uncomfortable with that. They want to be 'happy all the time'; and in the setting of a small-group meeting or Sabbath school class will sometimes try to lighten a serious mood by making light-hearted comments.

Where someone is hurting, or where there is a confession of sin or need, this is highly inappropriate. But these times are more the exception than the rule. As the Psalmist wrote, *'Your presence fills me with joy and brings me pleasure for ever.'*[15] Joy and a spirit of celebration is normal for a worship setting, because in God's presence we see our lives, with all their difficulties, in proper perspective, and sometimes we can't help laughing aloud at what we see.

The point is that true worship comes from within the deepest part of our being, as we respond to what God is doing or saying among us. Let us not quench the work of the Spirit by denying the expression of sadness, joy, thanksgiving, adoration, or just appreciation for the way God is and what He has done for us.

In churches which encourage the expression of such emotions, it is not unusual for spontaneous applause to follow a particularly moving experience, such as a hymn of praise or a baptism. The applause is directed not to the performers, but to God. In a Spirit-led church, *'everything must be done in a proper and orderly way',*[16] but at the same time worshippers need the freedom to express themselves from the heart in worship. So the raising of a hand in harmony with the words of a song is not necessarily 'charismatic' and out of place, but an act of worship and very much *in* place. We should not give the impression that we disapprove of such things, lest we be found to be quenching the moving of the Spirit.

Loving relationships

Disciples of Jesus are also members of His family,[17] and as such can enjoy one another when they are together. The more abundant life in Christ includes the loving, committed relationships which can grow among believers. Schwartz's survey shows that growing churches are generally those of which the members can say, *'There is a lot of laughter in our church'!* But such communities of faith don't just happen; they are made.

One of the greatest challenges of living as Christians is to love one another as Christ has loved us.[18] That kind of love is possible only in a community where the Spirit of Christ dwells, and where believers understand the need to:

* spend sufficient time with one another;
* communicate with one another on an in-depth, personal level;
* know one another's hopes and fears as well as opinions; trust one another;
* be accountable to one another. Love, as we have seen, is a commitment to another person's spiritual growth, and a high level of mutual accountability facilitates this growth.

God's *agape* love is not so much warm, fuzzy feelings between people as the intention to do others good.

It follows that the kind of loving relationships Jesus asks for cannot happen in the traditional setting of church meetings, however well intentioned we may be. Most of us, and that includes pastors and elders, are able on a practical level to develop such relationships with only a dozen or so other individuals outside our own immediate family. While we can be loving towards all, we can build caring, supportive relationships only with a smaller number, and that is probably one of the main reasons why Jesus chose only twelve out of the multitude who followed Him actually to be *with* Him.

One of the greatest benefits of well-run small groups is that they build loving relationships between members and their friends. These authentic relationships serve as a persuasive witness to non-Christians who attend group meetings that there is life-changing power in the love of Christ.[19] But it

 is not only non-Christians who are impressed. It is not unusual to hear Christians say, 'I have been attending church for twenty years, but I have never been so close to other Christians as I am now in my small group.' Small groups really work, not least because the bottleneck of the 'big church' mentality is removed; the laity of the church become the ministers of the church; and the life-giving river of the Spirit can flow unhindered through the spiritual gifts He has given for the building up of the body of Christ.

Flexibility

This kind of flexibility has nothing to do with bending whichever way the wind blows, but everything to do with being a genuinely caring and responsive community. We're talking Spirit-led flexibility here, which makes all the difference between a rigid, programme-based ministry, and one that is sensitive and people-based. For example:

- If church members say they don't attend Sabbath school because they don't find the Sabbath school lessons helpful, the flexible church will offer alternatives for the Bible study period which they will find attractive.
- Which is more important in the Sabbath school class – to get through the lesson study from Sunday to Friday, or to minister effectively to the needs of the members of the study group? The answer is obvious. So if a class member indicates during the study that she is experiencing difficulty in her life, Spirit-led flexibility will cause the class

130

leader to suspend the study and give however much time is necessary for the class to minister to that member through prayer and loving concern. Weeks later, she will remember that experience far better than the Bible

study. (Of course, there is a downside if this practice is pursued regularly. In that event the needs of the majority give way to those of a minority. If the same person is demanding attention week after week then, clearly, the idea is being abused.)

- As Christians we have different needs and different ways of expressing ourselves. My future church must be flexible enough to accommodate as much variety of taste and expression as is practical, but it should not be offended if a group of its members choose to move to another church to worship because it is more 'their style'.

- If the mid-week prayer meeting is no longer as well-attended as it once was, instead of blaming the television, or the church members for their lack of spirituality, it may be better to ask: 'What is God saying to us here? Where is He leading us?' Perhaps the needs of the church could be better served by many small groups meeting in one anothers' homes at different times and on different days, and the 'prayer meeting' being closed entirely.

Positive attitude to change

The God we worship is just as much the Creator today as He ever was. He is therefore well able to meet the changing needs of a changing world in all sorts of creative ways. In order to be in touch with the work of His Spirit, it is important that we regularly examine the wheels we are running on to make sure that we are not stuck in a rut, or, even worse, a dried-out river bed. Yesterday's church cannot be tomorrow's church. It is unreasonable to expect people who live in the world of the year 2000+ all week to switch easily to a 1950s world on Sabbaths. What we do as a church and how we do it must be in touch with the people we are called to serve, just as the Spirit is.

Leith Anderson describes the successful future church as *'the renewing church'* which is always going through a process of change and which *'throws out the worst and retains the best',* a process which *'guarantees both stability and relevance.'* He then summarizes by saying that *'the renewing church . . . must be bound by the cause of Jesus Christ but open to new ideas and changing structures. Distinction must be made between moral absolutes and cultural relatives. . . Change and challenge should not be threatening but recognized as part of the process. Leaders must keep calling the organization and its people back to the Lordship of Jesus Christ and the standards of the Bible while challenging people to grow and innovate within the Biblical boundaries. Fulfilling the mission is always more important than perpetuating traditions.'*[20]

As we have already noted, Adventist 'sacred cows' are more common than they ought to be for a church that began as it did in the upheavals and reforms of the Second Advent awakening of the early 1800s. The pioneers were forced to leave the churches they had attended for years, and were even rejected by their families for embracing the strange 'new light' of William Miller and his fellow preachers. They viewed tradition as belonging to Babylon, and many viewed the early attempts to organize the Seventh-day Adventist church as a mistake. They saw themselves as a movement being led by the Spirit of Truth who was sent to lead them into *'all the truth'*.[21] Even the formulation of a simple list of beliefs which they held in common was considered dangerous at first, lest it limit their ability to move forward and grow in their understanding of truth.

My future church needs to be in step with the spirit of the pioneers, but not necessarily all their methods. I would love my church to be known for

- its innovative worship services,
- the high value it places on creativity among its members,
- its general love of life and sense of adventure,
- the way it challenges and encourages individual believers to grow constantly in their personal lives,
- its ability to respond quickly to the need for new ministries for both believers and seekers,
- its humble recognition that it is on a journey of learning and discovery, and therefore does not have all the answers.

All-member ministry

You don't have to have a degree in maths to know that if the majority of the members of a church love their Lord and one another, and are engaged in ministry according to their spiritual giftedness, they will do a better overall job than an overworked pastor and half a dozen elders could ever do. But it takes special insight to understand why it is so imperative that the majority should become involved in this way. You have probably heard it before, but here it is again:

*'When we have entire, wholehearted consecration to the service of Christ, God will recognise the fact by an outpouring of His Spirit without measure; **but this will not be while the largest portion of the church are not labourers together with God'**.*[22]

Without question, the real potential for the unprecedented growth of my future church lies in the gifts-based ministry of all its members. This is the bottom line of the Spirit's plan for the successful completion of the work which Christ began, and deserves a full chapter all to itself!

[1] John 4:14.

[2] John 7:37-39; John 14:16, 17.

[3] Ephesians 3:17-19.

[4] Luke 11:13.

[5] 1 Corinthians 14:40.

[6] The structure of the New Testament church was close to what we would now call the Cell Model, which combines the advantages of small-group ministry (cell) with large-group ministry (celebration). Leadership was based on the 'Jethro principle', described in Exodus 18, with the apostles in Jerusalem at its head. The genius of this system was that every believer could be involved in ministry, and large numbers of converts could rapidly be absorbed into the church.

[7] 1 Peter 2:9 speaks of the priesthood of all believers and their participation in ministry.

[8] C. Mervyn Maxwell, 'Discovering the Power of Pentecost', Adventist Review (Hagerstown, MD: Review and Herald, 1999), special issue: "Time to Seek the Lord," page 334.

[9] William M. Easum, page 125.

[10] 2 Corinthians 3:17.

[11] John 10:10.

[12] Christian A. Schwartz, page 27.

[13] John 4:22-24, The Living Bible.

[14] Source unknown.

[15] Psalm 16:11.

[16] 1 Corinthians 14:40.

[17] Luke 8:21; Galatians 6:10; Ephesians 2:19.

[18] John 15:12.

[19] John 13:35.

[20] Leith Anderson, Dying for Change (Minneapolis, Minnesota: Bethany House Publishers, 1998), page 136.

[21] John 16:13 (This text is listed thirty times in the Comprehensive Index to the Writings of Ellen G. White vol. 1, page 123.

[22] Ellen G. White, Evangelism, page 699 (emphasis mine).

Chapter Eight

Where Are All the Ministers?

Every-member ministry

'God's work is retarded by criminal unbelief in His power to use the common people to carry forward His work successfully.' [1]

According to at least one very reliable source, the future looks bright, and my future church can be a part of it. As John describes it: *'After this I saw another angel coming down out of heaven. He had great authority, and his splendour brightened the whole earth.'* [2] The Bible assures us that before Christ returns God will arrange for one last, loving invitation to be sent through His church to every living person on Earth to prepare for that event. That invitation will be the same as it always was – the everlasting Gospel. But it will be delivered with such illuminating clarity and convicting power that it will figuratively bathe the entire globe in glory. When will it happen? It's an open secret as Jesus Himself explained: *'"And this Good News about the Kingdom will be preached through all the world for a witness to all mankind; and then the end will come."'* [3]

It couldn't be much simpler than that! The trouble with simple statements, though, is that we read them, agree with them, quickly move on to something more difficult – and fail to grasp the profound implications of what we have just read.

Apparently, Christ will not come until and unless the population of the entire world at that time has been made aware of the event. That enormous task has to be started and finished within a single generation, which at the present time consists of eight billion people! Incredible! So a far more important question than 'when will this happen?' is 'how will it happen?'

Obviously none of us knows, because the work of penetrating human hearts and changing human lives for the better always was and always will be God's work, not ours. Moreover, He has a thousand ways of working which we know nothing about. But we do know one thing: He has chosen to make His own work dependent to some extent on our co-operation. If global evangelization were simply a matter of informing people about the basis facts of the Gospel, He could accomplish that through angel messengers alone, with maybe some use of television, radio, the Internet and the world-wide web! But there is clearly more to it than that. God uses people to reach people. So a third question has to be, 'Where are all the ministers?' We already have the answer!

'The great outpouring of the Spirit of God, which lightens the earth with His glory, will not come until we have an enlightened people, that know by experience what it means to be labourers with God. When we have entire, wholehearted consecration to the service of Christ, God will recognise the fact by an outpouring of His Spirit without measure; **but this will not be while the largest portion of the church are not labourers together with God'.**[4]

The Holy Spirit, all-powerful and universally present though He is, does not do what only He can do without the co-operation of Christians – not just pastors, evangelists and Bible workers, but faithful believers who attend your church and my church faithfully each week. Not just a few believers, but the majority. There can be no bright future without them. They are so crucial to the whole operation that I felt obliged to repeat that inspired statement which closed the last chapter.

It really is a remarkable statement! It means it's really true that "many hands make light work". Let's look a little closer and hear what it is actually saying and what it is not saying:

- It is *not* saying that more church members should do door-to-door surveys or distribute Bible study invitation cards.
- It is *not* saying that more members should learn how to give Bible studies.
- It is *not* saying that more members should attend Sabbath school or prayer meeting.
- It is *not* even saying that more members should pay tithe or give more generous offerings.

All of these things and many more may be involved along the way, but they are not *the* issue. After all, anyone, converted or unconverted, could do them and no one would know the difference. The statement is saying something much more important:

- It *is* saying that God's Spirit will come when we have *'an enlightened people'*.
- It *is* saying that enlightened people are those who *'know **by experience** what it means to be labourers together with God'*.
- It *is* saying that we shall have this experience as the result of *'entire, wholehearted consecration to the service of Christ'*.
- It *is* saying that there can be no final, great outpouring of

137

the Spirit of God, without the majority of members (presumably world-wide simultaneously), being involved in this level and quality of involvement.

Every Member a Minister of Christ

Your conclusions on all this may be different from mine on the details, but we can probably agree in that what we are looking at here in principle is a very close connection between Jesus and His church. Its members are so closely identified with Him that He can think through them, speak through them, and act through them. In this sense every member becomes His minister. Through their spiritual gifts, His Spirit continues His work as if Christ were here in person. The difference is that the result is far more extensive, just as Jesus promised.[5]

The idea of every-member ministry is not a new one. It was the basis of ministry in the New Testament church. It was also the basis of church ministry during the first few decades of the Advent movement and the reason for its phenomenal growth during that time.[6] Since that time, to the extent it has been understood and applied in different parts of the world, the church has flourished. Unfortunately over the years the terms 'laity' and 'ministry' have parted company. 'Laity' has become the designated term for church members, and 'ministry' has been used mainly in reference to the clergy, the professional pastors of the church. Now it is time to put them together again and talk about 'the ministry of the laity' in the proper sense of the phrase. Paul Stevens puts it this way:

*'Laity is a word derived from the Greek word for "people" and it means all the people of God (1 Peter 2:9-10). **It is a term of incredible honour**. In Christ all the laity become ministering persons. They are not merely the recipients of*

*ministry from pastors, missionaries and theologians. The laity **are** the ministers. They are the means by which Jesus continues to minister in the world in the power of His Spirit. And the job of pastors is not to do the ministry themselves, but "to equip all the saints for the work of ministry." (Ephesians 4:11-12, RSV).*[7] *– emphasis mine.*

We have yet to see what will happen when we *fully* understand and embrace this wonderful truth.

From Theory to Practice

How can we move more closely towards this New Testament model of ministry? How can my future church develop and deploy its amazing ministry potential more fully and effectively than my present church is doing? It seems to me there are two things to consider here:

- The way we think about lay ministry
- Our ministry structure.

1. The way we think about lay ministry

For the past thirty years or so in particular, there have been encouraging signs that as a denomination we have not been satisfied with the status quo of Adventist lay ministry. For example, numerous publications, from Gottfried Oosterwal's *Mission Possible* published in 1972 to Rex Edwards' classic *Every Member a Minister* in 1985[8] and Russell Burrill's trilogy on the topic published between 1993 and 1997,[9] plus articles in our church papers have challenged us to think again about how we think of ministry.

Nevertheless, the way we actually *do* ministry in and through the local church reflects the traditional way we still think about it. For the majority, lay ministry is limited to perceptions such as these:

- Ministry is the work of the pastor of the church or the one holding church office.
- Lay ministry means holding church office.
- Church members minister by supporting the pastor in *his* or *her* ministry or by helping the church at large to do its work (e.g. through church offerings, Ingathering, etc.).
- Church members can minister by doing more challenging tasks, such as giving Bible studies, teaching a Sabbath school class, and preaching, but only a few are competent in these areas.
- There are three 'levels' of ordination to ministry: one for pastors, one for elders and one for deacons. Those who are not pastors, elders or deacons are not ordained to the ministry.

Real ministry is . . . simply people helping other people to experience the reality of God in their lives. Peter, who had been with Jesus right from the start, summed up His ministry this way:

'*"You know the message he [God] sent to the people of Israel, proclaiming the Good News of peace through Jesus Christ, who is Lord of all . . . You know about Jesus of Nazareth and how God poured out on him the Holy Spirit and power. He went everywhere, doing good and healing all who were under the power of the Devil, for God was with him."*'[10]

The ministry of sharing the Good News as Jesus shared it is now the work of the church, and it has been given to '*all believers in Christ to the end of time*',[11] not just to pastors.

Gifts-based ministry. One thing is obvious about the work of the church: it's bigger than we are. Even if the church were a thousand times bigger than it is and our budgets were calculated in billions rather than millions, we would still face an impossible task. We can't even convert a single soul or nurture a disciple, never mind evangelize a country. Church work is supernatural work. And, fortunately, Jesus has provided supernatural resources that are more than adequate. Those resources are the gifts of the Spirit, for *'it was he who "gave gifts to mankind"; he appointed some to be apostles, others to be prophets, others to be evangelists, others to be pastors and teachers. **He did this to prepare all God's people for the work of Christian service, in order to build up the body of Christ.'**[12]*

Ministry (i.e. 'service'), then, is the work of the Spirit through believers, and all believers are included in His work, for *'the Spirit's presence is shown in some way in each person for the good of all.'*[13] The purpose of the gifts of the Spirit is to 'build up' or to 'edify' the body of Christ. A brief glance at the many 'body-building' texts in Scripture shows that such edification is the process of helping people to grow towards spiritual maturity. As demonstrated in the early church, the exercise of spiritual gifts also resulted in the rapid numerical growth of the church through evangelism.

The effectiveness of the church's ministry is therefore dependent on the recognition and development of the gifts the Spirit has given to all the members of the body, and their willingness and ability to respond to His direction concerning their use. We can only speculate about the consequences when the members of my future church *'stir up (rekindle the embers of, fan the flame of, and keep burning)'*[14] the gifts God has already given us, and *'earnestly desire'*[15] the gifts most needed for our mission. As Christian Schwartz observes:

'When Christians serve in their area of gifting, they generally function less in their own strength and more in the

141

Spiritual Body-Building in the Early Church

- **Romans 14:19** So then, we must always aim at those things that bring peace and that help to strengthen [build up] one another.
- **Romans 15:2** We should all please our brothers for their own good, in order to build them up in the faith.
- **1 Corinthians 14:12** Since you are eager to have the gifts of the Spirit, you must try above everything else to make greater use of those which help to build up the church.
- **Ephesians 2:22** In union with him you too are being built together with all the others into a place where God lives through his Spirit.
- **Ephesians 4:29** Do not use harmful words, but only helpful words, the kind that build up and provide what is needed.
- **Colossians 2:7** Keep your roots deep in him, build your lives on him, and become stronger in your faith, as you were taught.
- **1 Thessalonians 5:11** And so encourage one another and help [build up] one another, just as you are now doing.
- **1 Peter 2:5** Come as living stones, and let yourselves be used in building [i.e. edifying] the spiritual temple, where you will serve as holy priests to offer spiritual and acceptable sacrifices to God through Jesus Christ.
- **Jude 20** But you, my friends, keep on building yourselves up on your most sacred faith.

power of the Holy Spirit. Thus ordinary people can accomplish the extraordinary! . . .

'An interesting corollary result of our research was the discovery that no factor seems to influence the contentedness of Christians more than whether they are utilizing their gifts or not.'[16]

Clearly, we still have some growing to do in the way we think about ministry! But I trust that my future church will at least be able to agree that:

- Ministry is not a human activity but a divine/human activity.
- The members of the church are the ministers of the church. As a member of the church the pastor can and should share in that ministry, but he or she is not *the* minister. Members are ministers every bit as much as he or she is.
- Christian ministry takes many forms, from feeding the hungry to preaching to giving Bible studies to encouraging fellow believers, but its purpose is always to bring God near to others in the hope that lives will be changed and the church 'built up'.
- Ordination or calling to ministry is bestowed equally on every believer at baptism. Christ's baptism marked the beginning of His formal ministry and He was equipped for ministry by the descent of the Holy Spirit. His baptism was a 'sample' of our baptism. Church ordination by the laying on of hands to set apart certain persons for certain tasks should not convey the idea that their calling is more important than that of others.

2. Our ministry structure

It's a chicken and egg situation: our thinking about ministry is related to the way the church is organized and structured for ministry. Which came first – our thinking or our system – is hardly the point. The point is that just as traditional views of lay ministry have limited the involvement of members in ministry, so our present ministry system may also be standing in the way of progress.

As with our thinking about ministry, so with our ministry structure – there have been some encouraging developments in recent years. Many local congregations are developing ministry systems that are tailored more to local ministry needs than to the traditional Adventist blueprint. Despite this, however, the ministry system of most local (British) Adventist churches is still based primarily on:

A. Departments. For good reasons the church is organized departmentally (i.e. Youth, Sabbath school, Stewardship, Community Services, Personal Ministries, etc.). The system has served and still serves us well, but it has certain limitations:

- It may not have room for every kind of spiritual gift present in the church.
- It may have the effect of creating conflict and competition for available resources rather than teamwork between departments.
- It can create an artificial distinction between members who are seen to be involved in the church and those who are not.
- Because it is a top-down system (i.e. General Conference to local church) it is somewhat inflexible. Every congregation is expected to replicate it within the possible limitations of its size. So that in very small congregations there are sometimes more offices to be filled than there are members to fill them, while in large congregations there are far more capable and willing leaders than there are leadership roles to give them.
- Because it is a top-down system, it tends not to be based on local ministry needs in the church or community.

B. Programmes. Adventists can boast some of the best programmes there are. As good as they are, however, if they are not tailor-made to the needs of the people for whom they are intended, their effectiveness will be limited. Programmes tend to create a 'one-size-fits-all' approach to ministry, unintentionally ignoring the large and many differences in local needs. For example, one Sabbath school lesson topic is provided for the world church in the cause of world-church unity. The question is, does it have the same relevance for Eskimos as for Australians, for parents of young children as for senior members facing retirement?

A second weakness of a programme-based ministry is that it tends to make us dependent on available resources. Rather than create new and evolving ministries for a specific local situation, we tend to limit ourselves to existing materials for Revelation seminars, marriage and parenting workshops, or five-session courses on healthy-living. Adventists are often reluctant to use the much wider range of non-Adventist programme materials that are available, and fail to use the creative gifts of local church members to develop new ministry tools designed specifically for the local situation.

C. Buildings. We say that the church is people, and that ministry should happen where those people are, but we still tend to make the church building the centre of our ministry. Local congregations which do not own their own property are likely to feel incomplete, as if they have not yet 'arrived'. To use a school hall or a non-Adventist church building for church services is generally seen to be a hindrance to ministry. It follows that all available money is set aside for the future purchase of a church building, while fund-raising activities consume much time and energy of the members. 'When we have our own building we will be able to do so much more' is the sort of sentiment one can expect to hear when visiting such congregations.

A building-based ministry may be good in some situations. In others it may limit members in ministry to those who are involved in church-based activities. It may also restrict the effectiveness of the church in the community if local people are reluctant to come to the church building.

This 'post modern' generation, as we have seen, is highly mobile. Even entire housing estates can pass their sell-by date. Within a few short years a part of town which was highly desirable as a place to live in when it was first built can become run-down, very undesirable. Instead of moving in, people move away; shops close; the local park and play area are neglected; and churches which once thrived struggle to stay open. Churches must keep up with people, not just their needs, and that applies to buildings, too.

The best ministry system is . . . the one that best serves the needs of local church members and non-church members. Ministry is service, response to human need; so the best ministry system is the one which best facilitates that response.

Departments, programmes and buildings are all good, in their proper place. But they are all means to an end (which is service), not an end in themselves. It follows that if a department, for whatever reason, is no longer serving the purpose for which it was created, it should not exist in the local church. Likewise, if a building is more of a hindrance than a help to ministry, the congregation should look for an alternative base. Perhaps my future church should see its building, if it owns one, more as a community centre than simply a place of worship. And if it is a community centre, it should look like one and operate like one.

The ministry system of the New Testament church is difficult, if not impossible, to improve on. Jerusalem and the Middle East in the first century AD might have differed in some respects from London and the Western World in the twenty-first century, but some things are similar. Then, as now, the prevailing culture was materialistic and largely pagan. Then as now the church needed a system of ministry which was simple, yet able to handle sudden, explosive growth. Then, as now, new believers from many different backgrounds needed to be lovingly cared for, thoroughly taught, and quickly trained for ministry. Jesus Himself drew many striking parallels between the time preceding the fall of Jerusalem and the time preceding His Second Advent. Could it be that the New Testament church's system for ministry should be ours as well?

Author and church-growth consultant William Beckham, in his excellent book *The Second Reformation,*[17] argues that the success of the early church was due as much to its system of ministry as to its members' readiness for ministry. Both the members and the system were divinely ordained for ministry; both were taught and modelled by Jesus, especially through the calling and instructing of the twelve. The Holy Spirit needed both to be able to accomplish what He did at Pentecost and afterwards. Beckham also argues that the later apostasy of the church was twofold: a departure from the true teaching of Scripture, and a departure from its God-ordained ministry system. The thesis of the book is that God's true church today can go only so far and no further in the accomplishment of its mission, if it concerns itself only with the restoration of true biblical teaching but ignores the system. Hence the title. God is leading His church to a *second reformation,* a return to the New Testament model of ministry, to enable her to complete her commission – the Gospel to all the world in one generation.

The most important characteristic of the ministry system of the apostolic church was its combination of small-group ministry with large-group ministry. While the believers participated in large gatherings at the temple or other public places for the purpose of worship or evangelism, it is clear that they also met regularly in the more informal and intimate setting of one another's homes. For all practical purposes, that is where the church grew. That is where believers gathered for prayer, cared for one another, and discipled and trained new converts. Large meetings were also important however, when persecution did not prevent their taking place: they provided the best setting for celebratory worship, inspired teaching and the overall co-ordination of their mission. Like the two oars of a rowing boat, these two equally important parts of their ministry system complemented one another. The church went where it was supposed to go. It did not go round in circles.

Small-group ministry in my future church will be vital to its success, just as it was vital to the success of the early church. Small groups are so vital that they have been called 'cells', since the cell is the basic building block of every living thing. It's the one thing that daisies and dinosaurs have in common! All living  things, however large or small, function and grow only because of what happens within the cells of which they are made. The church is also a living thing. It is the body of Christ, and every member is a part of it, ministering to and through the body according to his or her giftedness.

Small groups bring Christians into close relationship with one another as nothing else can. They complement and support rather than replace the programmes, departments and building of the church at large, but their principal concern is growth . . .

⸙ growth in our relationship with God,
⸙ growth in our relationship with one another,
⸙ numerical growth through evangelism.

So important is the role of small groups to the growth of today's churches that of the eight characteristics Schwartz identified as common to all growing churches, he concluded that *'if we were to identify any one principle as the most important – even though our research shows that the interplay of all basic elements is important – then without a doubt, it would be the multiplication of small groups.'*[18]

My future church needs to take this observation seriously. It needs to understand that small groups are not a programme, not a gimmick, not a passing fashion, but a divinely ordained system of ministry. They form the basic structure for a people-based church in which Christ dwells and through which the Holy Spirit works. Through small groups or cells, church-wide, gifts-based, every-member ministry can be organized, intentional, and inclusive of all. As in the early church, they:

- enable members to identify and develop their spiritual gifts for ministry,
- enable every member to become a minister, building others up in Christ,
- provide an environment in which non-Christian friends can see for themselves what a true Christian community is like, and be exposed to the Gospel in living form,
- facilitate the development of loving, supportive relationships between group members,
- prepare the church for the glorious finishing of her mission on Earth.

In a word, small groups can make Christian community a reality in the church, in a way that would be impossible through larger, more formal congregational meetings alone. Where there is Christian community, there is also unity of the New Testament kind in which *'the largest portion of the church . . . know by experience what it means to be labourers together with God.'* And where there is that kind of unity, the way is prepared for *'the great outpouring of the Spirit'* to come.[19]

Every Christian is . . .

Created for ministry (Ephesians 2:10)
Called into ministry (1 Peter 2:9, 10)
Gifted for ministry (1 Peter 4:10)
Authorized for ministry (Matthew 28:18-20)
Commanded to minister (Matthew 20:26-28)
To be *prepared* for ministry (Ephesians 4:11, 12)
Needed for ministry (1 Corinthians 12:27)
Accountable for ministry (Colossians 3:23)
To be *rewarded* for ministry (Colossians 3:24)

Refocusing the ministry of the church

Mobilizing the members of our church for ministry is clearly not an option. It is no exaggeration to say that virtually everything depends on it, from our survival and growth as a church to the successful completion of our mission before Christ returns. It is a matter of urgency, therefore, that we build a more gifts-based ministry than we have at the present time, and that we return to the more biblical structure of church described above. Unless we do, it is very doubtful that we will ever realize the full potential of every-member ministry.

Having said that, however, we must also realize that every-member ministry will not happen simply by changing definitions and structures. The ways of Jesus are always radically different from what we are used to, and His call to ministry is no exception. The new wine of the Gospel requires new wineskins to carry it, not just old ones that have been patched up. We need a new mindset, a new way of thinking about the context in which ministry takes place. This includes not only the question of 'who' Christ's ministers are, but where, when and how such ministry should take place.

- **The 'Where' of ministry.** Since Christians *are* 'the King's priests'[20] – they don't just *do* priestly work; they *are* priests wherever they happen to be. In the same sense, all believers are ministers of Christ, wherever they go – their ministry is not limited to a particular place. Believers are just as much the ministers of Christ at school or college, workplace or home, as they are in the place of worship, probably more so, in fact, since that is where they spend most of their time and have the greatest potential influence. Perhaps we need to recognize better than we do that it is not just the place of worship that is sacred – wherever we are in the service of God is also holy ground.

- **The 'When' of ministry.** Ministry is not something that happens only during a worship service or for an hour on Sabbath afternoons while we are knocking on people's doors. We are ministers of Jesus twenty-four hours a day, 365 days a year. Our particular spiritual gifts may mean that we (and others) are more aware of our ministry opportunities at some times more than others, but we need to be 'available' for service at any time, as the Spirit may lead or give opportunity. If we could embrace this idea, what a difference it would make to the way we view the working week, and the more menial duties of life. We would be able to say with Mark Greene, *Thank God it's Monday!*[21] After all, Monday for most of us is the start of the working week and it is where we spend the working week, whether in the classroom, hospital ward or office, that we probably have most influence, because that's where we spend most of our time.

And remember, all our time is sacred. Is Sabbath more sacred than Monday? Maybe it is, maybe it isn't. Sabbath is distinctly *different* from the other days of the week, but Jesus is just as much Lord of all my time – yes, even Mondays – as He is Lord of the Sabbath.

ꙮ **The 'How' of ministry.** In one sense, Christian ministry is not something that we do, but something that Christ does through us, wherever, whenever, and for whomever He chooses. We don't have to worry, therefore, about turning every conversation we have to religious topics. We simply need to be sensitive to the needs and possibilities around us, and to be responsive to what God is doing (or not doing) in any particular situation. He is well able to create opportunities for witness or service, if we are available and willing to be used by Him.

Every profession a calling. If the concept of Christian ministry described above is true, it is difficult to escape the conclusion that every profession is a calling, and every job a divine appointment. It is a serious mistake to think that only pastors and Bible workers have sacred callings – we all do! The places in which we are called to minister may be as different as the gifts for ministry we have been given, but all Christian service, all Christian ministry, is equally sacred. So when we encourage young people to 'train for the ministry', let's not limit that encouragement to those who go to study theology to become our future pastors. Whatever their choice of profession, all young people should be encouraged to prepare themselves for ministry. (Perhaps our training colleges could develop a one-year intensive 'ministry in the marketplace' course for young adults to precede or follow their university training.)

Seven Laws of Evangelism

1. **Law of abundance** (John 10:10). The best gift we can give to others is to live the abundant life of joy and freedom ourselves.

2. **Law of prayer** (John 6:44). People come to Christ because the Father 'draws' them. Through prayer we ask God to connect us with those He is already calling.

3. **Law of preparedness** (1 Peter 3:15). We are each responsible for developing our own preparedness.

4. **Law of proximity** (Matthew 5:13). We must mix with and come close to people to be effective.

5. **Law of process** (Mark 4:26-29). Leading people to faith is not an event, but is like putting together the pieces of a jigsaw puzzle. Decisions come when people see the whole picture.

6. **Law of love** (Ephesians 4:15). 'Speaking the truth' is effective only in the context of a loving relationship.

7. **Law of spiritual leadings** (John 16:13). It is the Spirit's work to lead people into truth. We must be sensitive to His promptings which lead us to opportunities for witness.

It follows that it is not just those who feel called to study theology in preparation for denominational service who need to pray for God to guide them: every believer has that need. Those who are preparing for a career in teaching or com-

"AS THE FATHER SENT ME, SO I SEND YOU"

puter science, nursing or child care, need God's guidance just the same.

The important thing is to be where God wants us to be, doing what He wants us to do. However good a pastor may be at his particular job, he cannot relate to a physician as well as a fellow physician can. No one understands the stresses of a managing director better than another managing director. A woman who teaches at university half her life and cares for her family the other half identifies best with other women in similar situations. A construction worker speaks the language of other construction workers better than anyone else, and so on.

How important, then, that it is not salary level, working conditions, company perks or family heritage that determines our career choice or the place where we pursue that career, but Providence. Let's encourage children and young people still at school to start praying early about their career choices, and the educational options best suited to those choices. AYS committees please take note when planning programmes!

Ordained to ministry. As has already been noted, the significance of the baptism of Jesus lies partly in the fact that His ministry of teaching, preaching and healing formally began at that time. Likewise the visible descent of the dove symbolized the special anointing of the Holy Spirit to equip Him for that ministry. Since His baptism is an example for us to follow, it is reasonable to believe that what happened at His baptism also happens at ours.[22] There may be no visible manifestation of the Spirit's presence at such times, but we can be sure that as we commit ourselves to His service He comes to equip us for that service. As Peter explained in his Pentecost sermon, *"Each one of you must turn away from his sins and be baptized in the name of Jesus Christ, so that your sins will be forgiven; and you will receive God's gift, the Holy Spirit."*[23]

So why do we publicly ordain pastors, elders and deacons by the laying on of hands at special, non-baptismal ordination services? We do it because this is the way the New Testament church did it. Every member is ordained to be a minister of Christ at the time of baptism: but particular indi-

154

viduals are 'set apart' by the church to designated roles by the laying on of hands. This does not make their ministry superior in any way to that of other non-ordained believers. The work of the Sabbath school teacher, the church treasurer or the Personal Ministries leader is no less important than the work of the deacon, or the pastor for that matter. So why don't we ordain every member to ministry in a similar way?

My guess is that if the New Testament church had had a more highly developed structure for ministry which included these other offices, they would probably have ordained the individuals who served in those offices too. I am not suggesting that we should start ordaining every church officer recommended by the nominating committee. I am simply suggesting that we recognize every ministry as equally sacred, whether it is done 'officially' within the organizational structure of the church, or 'unofficially' outside that structure. I like the idea that the ordination of pastors, elders and deacons symbolically represents the ordination of the whole body of the church to the entirety of its ministry at that particular time. We need to know that all of us are equally the ministers of Christ.

Equipping members for ministry

If my future church is to be a lay-ministered church, and if lay ministry is as crucial to its survival and growth as it appears to be, it is only reasonable to suggest that we should pour all our available resources into it. Here, more than anywhere else, is where we need to concentrate our attention, time, energy and money, and in the following areas in particular:

a. **Training members for ministry.** If we are serious about the ministry of the laity, we must get serious about the training of the laity for their ministry. Think about it.

Pastors employed by the church are given between three and six years of formal training for their responsibilities, but no formal training is required for church elders, even though they take the pastor's place in his or her absence. Teachers in secular State schools have undergone rigorous training both in the university classroom and on teaching practice, but no formal training is required of Sabbath school teachers who deal with eternal realities.

More church members participate 'up-front' in worship services and other public meetings these days. This is good if they are trained and competent, bad if they are not. If my future church is going to tap into its every-member ministry potential, it is going to have to take training more seriously, just as those first Adventists did. Remember, *'Every church should be a training school for Christian workers. Its members should be taught how to give Bible readings, how to conduct and teach Sabbath-school classes, how best to help the poor and to care for the sick, how to work for the unconverted . . . There should not only be teaching, but actual work under experienced instructors.'*[24] Who will these *'experienced instructors'* be? They could be any of the following:

- The local church pastor.
- The pastor from another district who has the necessary skills.
- Conference/Union departmental leaders or officers.
- Experienced and skilled church members.
- Qualified Christians from other denominations who have skills or experience not found in any of the above.

The pastor's role. Although there are many individuals who can serve the church as *'experienced instructors'*, it is clearly the pastor's role to organize this training. In the church where every member really is a minister, the pastor is no longer 'the minister' of the church, but the teacher/trainer/facilitator of the church's ministry. Of course he or she continues to be *a* minister of the church, for the pastor is also a member of the laity (one of the people of God) and should do the work of ministry along with every other lay person. But the pastor's primary task is to help believers to find their unique place within the body, identifying their ministry gifts, and arranging suitable training for them. As we have been told, *'The best help that ministers [pastors] can give the members of our churches is not sermonizing, but planning work for them.'*[25]

'They are not only to minister to the people, but to teach them to minister. They should not only give instruction in right principles, but educate their hearers to impart these principles. Truth that is not lived, that is not imparted, loses its life-giving power, its healing virtue.'[26]

Some church leaders have expressed the fear that if we were to develop a lay ministry like this, pastors would be out of a job; The exact opposite is true. If we were to develop a lay ministry like this, pastors would be *into* their job and, having found their calling, they would find their work more fulfilling and less draining than before. No more pastoral burnout!

A good pastor is . . . Well, it's interesting how we define a good pastor, isn't it? If the pastor preaches well, visits regularly, wins new converts, takes care of baby dedications, weddings and funerals, and develops good relationships with leaders in the community, the church is happy. I wonder if the Lord of the church is as happy with our definition as we are? Recently I was disturbed to read that *'no minister should be measured by his ability as a speaker.'*[27] As important as preaching is to Adventist church life, as much as we enjoy a good sermon, and as much as many pastors enjoy preaching, the speaking ability of the pastor is not as important as perhaps we have made it. It's far more important for pastors to teach lay people to preach and work for God. This is their highest calling. If you find that somewhat upsetting, so do I. If I had my time over again, there are some things I would do differently! Hopefully, my future church will get this one right.

b. **Resourcing members for ministry.** Ministry is people helping people, but often the help that is needed is costly, in terms of money as well as time. One-to-one visitation in people's homes may not require much in the way of financial resources, but public programmes often do. High quality youth, health or family-oriented community programmes, or public evangelism done with excellence can be expensive ventures, especially in this high-technology world. Well-trained lay members involved in such ministry will need to be adequately funded, either by the local church or the conference. This may mean that we spend less on evangelistic programmes led by pastors and professional evangelists (except where they are entering new areas or planting new churches), but in the long term it will prove to be the best way of using our financial resources.

c. **Empowering members for ministry.** Providing training and resources for ministry is one thing. Allowing members to run with the vision is another. But if we are going to emphasize spiritual gifts as the future basis for ministry, it's essential that we give permission and make provision for everyone to use their gifts. As William Easum says,

'Each person is a unique gift from God with a unique

ministry to share with the world. Helping each person find that gift and live out that gift is the role of organization.[28]
Giving power to others for their ministry is not going to be easy for some of us, however, because it means surrendering power and control ourselves.

What does this empowerment process involve? Empowering some believers for their ministry may simply mean appointing them to existing programmes, positions or committees in the church and supporting and encouraging them in their endeavours. Empowering others might begin with the question, *'What gifts do you bring to the body of Christ, and how can we help you exercise them?'*

One recently planted lay-led church[29] encourages the formation of ministry teams as part of the empowerment process. Members who become aware of a ministry need, either inside or outside the church, and who feel able to respond to it, look for other members who will share their concern and vision. Once a rough plan of action has been thought through and enough individuals have been found to carry it out, the team present their proposal to the church at an appropriate meeting, and request permission to put that plan into action. Those who want to lead a ministry team are asked the following questions:

✦ Do you belong to a prayer group?
✦ Has the Holy Spirit led you to this? How do you know?
✦ How long are you going to do this ministry?
✦ Does it interfere with any other ministry?
✦ How will it be financed?

If the church is satisfied with the answers, and believes that the ministry will be conducted within the boundaries of its mission, vision and value statements,[30] the team are free to pursue their ministry without constant supervision from church leadership. At the same time, they are accountable to the church for what they do or do not do. The greater the freedom given, the greater the accountability required.

The empowerment process also involves efficiency. Especially in the case of ministry teams, which are usually (but not always) set up to meet an immediate, short-term need, it will be necessary for my future church to learn how to short-circuit the permission-giving process. Apart from the fact that we can kill enthusiasm by keeping people waiting to do what they want to do, we also need to respond to ministry needs as quickly as possible, because, as Easum points out, *'The shorter the time lag between discovering a spiritual need and the implementation of a response in the form of a new ministry, the more effective the church will be.'*[31]

Lay pastors in my future church

You may be surprised to learn, as I was when I first read about it, that early Adventists actually regarded the pastoral role as a local lay position and not a 'clergy' position. As Russell Burrill observes, *'They declared that the Scriptures recognized only two kinds of church officers: those called by God – the apostles and the evangelists, and those appointed by the church – the elders, the deacons and the pastors. The first two positions they held to be clergy positions; the last three they declared to be local and lay positions.'*[32]

One of the most exciting things about my future church is that the pastor, more likely than not, will be a lay pastor.[33] Even more likely, the leadership responsibilities of my future church will be shared among several lay pastors, each specializing in a particular area of church life, such as evangelism, nurture, worship and youth. Called by God and equipped by His Spirit to carry the burden of church leadership, these lay pastors will probably serve on a part-time basis as they will continue in their regular profession for their income (unless they are retired). One will probably be considered *the* pastor by the Conference, and will be directly responsible to the Conference as is any paid pastor.

A pastor who is employed by the Conference will possibly serve as a consultant to my church and perhaps a dozen other churches like it, visiting occasionally or by request. But for all practical purposes, the care and leadership of the church will be in the hands of dedicated lay men and women. I should like to think that there will be no pastoral duty which they are not empowered to fulfil, baptizing new converts, training believers for ministry, and conducting funerals.

Could it work? Is it practical? Considering that both the local congregations of the apostolic church and the early Adventist church were led by lay pastors, we can hardly say 'No'. The answer has to be 'Yes', but on two conditions:

1. Shared leadership. If full-time, paid pastors find it difficult to do all that is required of them, how could lay pastors survive, if they had to hold down full-time jobs in the market place as well? The answer is, they couldn't. Unless, of course, my future church operates on the 'Jethro principle' of shared and delegated leadership as described in Exodus 18:13-27. Given the fact that small-group leaders are already pastors in a limited sense of the word, and every believer is serving according to his gifts, is there any reason why the entire leadership of the church cannot be provided through its leaders of tens, fifties, and hundreds? If the membership of my future church is approximately one hundred (although the same principle applies equally well to much larger memberships) lay pastoral responsibilities would look like this:

Senior Lay Pastor
(leader of 100)

Assistant Lay Pastor   **Assistant Lay Pastor**
(leader of 50)   (leader of 50)

Small-Group Leaders   **Small-Group Leaders**
(leaders of 10)   (leaders of 10)

2. Adequate training. My future church must provide its lay pastors with both academic and practical training. Tailor-made academic training could be by part-time distance learning with an Adventist college or university to a minimum level of certificate or diploma, while hands-on experience could be provided by a professional pastor in the context of a small-group network. Once the potential pastor has demonstrated ability, first as a small-group leader and then as a supervisor of four or five other cells, and provided certain leadership gifts are evident, it would be a small step to investing him or her with the overall responsibility of leading the congregation. Where necessary, the cost of such training would need to be subsidized by local and/or Conference funds set aside for this purpose.

We have no choice. It seems to me that the development of such lay pastoral leadership is not optional – it is crucial to the successful completion of our mission as a church.

Since we believe that Christ's coming is near, my future church must begin to plan now for the unprecedented growth we believe will take place before that event. Tying professional pastors to one, two or three congregations is a luxury we can no longer afford. Apart from that, there are just not enough of them to care for all the new congregations we can expect to see being established.

We need hundreds of pastors where now we have only a few, so it is imperative that we begin now to identify the lay people whom God has called and equipped for greater responsibilities, and provide for their training. And what better way is there to begin, than to pray in earnest the one prayer that Jesus asked us to pray: *'"Pray to the owner of the harvest that he will send out workers to gather in his harvest."'*[34]

Youth in Ministry

While we may look within the membership of my future church as a whole for its lay leaders, it is likely that most, and probably the best, will be found among the youth. Ellen White said it first, of course: *'With such an army of workers as our youth, rightly trained, might furnish, how soon the message of a crucified, risen and soon-coming Saviour might be carried to the whole world!'*[35] Whether we older ones like it or not, the energy, strength, vision, creativity, and flexibility called for by the final work of God on Earth, which will be larger and more rapid than the Christian church has ever seen before, are more likely to be found among the youth than anywhere else.

Once before, when the people of God were on the verge of entering the Promised Land of Canaan, Providence chose a time when the vast majority were forty years of age or younger. While the overall responsibility of supervising that great movement was given to one who was older in years and more experienced in the things of God, the hard work of conquest, of local leadership and government, and of organizing the new nation, was in the hands of the young.

For different reasons from those which prevailed long ago, the world-wide average age of Christians is falling. In some countries as many as 50% of Seventh-day Adventists are under thirty years of age. Some may see this as a problem. We should see it as a wonderful advantage. Probably never before as a movement have we been blessed with so much skill, so much ambition, so much restlessness for change, so much influence, so much cross-cultural understanding, as we now have in the youth of the church. Those of older years will continue to have a crucial part to play in what lies before us. The work of directing, overseeing, counselling and supporting will continue to be the work of church elders, professional pastors and executive officers. But let the youth, once trained and tested, provide the leadership that only they can provide, at the cutting edge, where the action is.

Preparing youth for such leadership and service should surely be the primary purpose of the youth department of the church. Somehow, the original reason for its establishment seems to have been lost sight of, particularly in many local churches where the main function of the AYS appears to be to provide a weekly Sabbath afternoon programme, which does little or nothing to prepare young people for their future role.

Youth leadership, divinely chosen and equipped, was largely responsible for launching the Advent movement in the beginning, and there is little doubt that youth leadership will be just as responsible for the completion of its task.

In summary

From the beginning, the work of Christian ministry in all its forms has been the work of the laity, the people of God, and most of them have been plain, ordinary men and women like you and me. As Paul reminded the first believers at Corinth, *'From the human point of view few of you were wise or powerful or of high social standing. God purposely chose what the world considers nonsense in order to shame the wise, and he chose what the world considers weak in order to shame the powerful.'*[36]

The twelve apostles themselves, with the possible exception of Judas, saw themselves as ordinary people. Yet through them the church was organized and established as a force to be reckoned with in Jerusalem; and when the time came for the Good News to be spread more widely, it was other ordinary people who *'went everywhere, preaching the message.'*[37] Like you, they probably felt inadequate and ill-equipped. In fact, they might never have done what they did had it not been for the martyrdom of Stephen. Philip, one of seven humble deacons (i.e. servants), was among them, and was used mightily by the Holy Spirit as an evangelist. No doubt hundreds and thousands of other lay members of the church were used in a similar way.

Now it is time for that part of history to repeat itself. It is not just pastors who are called to ministry. All God's people, the laity, are called to be His ministers. Let all God's people get the message and share it, and the days of the church on Earth are numbered.

---

[1] Ellen G. White, *Review and Herald*, 16 July, 1895.
[2] Revelation 18:1.
[3] Matthew 24:14.
[4] E. G. White, *Review and Herald*, 21 July 1896.
[5] John 14:12.

[6] 'When it was basically a lay movement, possessing a clear understanding of the role of the laity, the Adventist church expanded very rapidly. In the first three decades after its inception, from 1870 to 1900, Seventh-day Adventist church membership increased rather spontaneously by 432.54 per cent. After 1901, when the Biblical concept of the laity became blurred and an ecclesiastical structure developed which centred around the "set apart minister", a sharp drop occurred in the missionary expansion of the church. In the three decades from 1900 to 1930 Adventist membership increased only 184.83 per cent.' Gottfried Oosterwal, Mission Possible (Nashville, Tennessee: Southern Publishing Association, 1972), page 107.

[7] Quoted in Merton B. Strommen, The Innovative Church (Minneapolis, U.S.A.: Augsburg), pages 142, 143.

[8] Rex D. Edwards, Every Member a Minister. (Hagerstown, MD, USA: General Conference of SDAs, 1995).

[9] Revolution in the Church (Fallbrook, California: Hart Research Center, 1993); Radical Disciples (1996); The Revolutionised Church of the 21st Century (1997).

[10] Acts 10:36, 38.

[11] Ellen G. White, The Desire of Ages, page 822.

[12] Ephesians 4:11, 12, emphasis mine.

[13] 1 Corinthians 12:7.

[14] 2 Timothy 1:6, Amplified Bible.

[15] 1 Corinthians 12:31, Amplified Bible.

[16] Schwartz, page 24.

[17] Houston, USA:Touch Publications, 1995.

[18] ibid., page 33.

[19] The unity of spirit between believers on the day of Pentecost was in fact the unity of wholehearted consecration to the service of Christ. See Ellen G. White, Acts of the Apostles, pages 36, 48.

[20] 1 Peter 2:9.

[21] This is the title of Mark Greene's excellent book about the priority of ministry in the workplace. (Bletchley, England: Scripture Union, 1997).

[22] In recognition of this fact, many congregations include some form of commissioning or dedication to service on the day of baptism. For example, while prayer is offered, church leaders and friends place their hands on the candidates.

[23] Acts 2:38.

[24] Ellen G. White, The Ministry of Healing, page 149.

[25] Ellen G. White, Testimonies, Vol. 6, page 49.

[26] Ellen G. White, The Ministry of Healing, page 149.

[27] Ellen G. White, Testimonies, Vol. 5, page 255.

[28] William Easum, page 123.

[29] Peoria,Il. SDA church.

[30] See Appendix C for sample of these.

[31] Easum, page 125.

[32] Russell Burrill, Rekindling a Lost Passion (Fallbrook, California: Hart Research Center, 1999), page 50.

[33] The term is used here to mean the leader of the local congregation. Of course an

effective small-group leader is in reality the pastor of the group, although we would not use the term 'pastor' in that way.

[34] Matthew 9:38.

[35] Ellen G. White, *Education,* page 271.

[36] 1 Corinthians 1:26, 27.

[37] Acts 8:4.

Chapter Nine

Welcome by Design

The User-Friendly church

'It can be immensely hard just walking through the door of a church.'

Yes, even for a Christian, and even for a church member from a different Adventist congregation, it can be very difficult walking through the doors of a new church for the first time. So what must it be like for those who have seldom or never been to church?

Maybe you know the answer to that question, because you once took that bold step yourself. Hopefully, the experience was not too difficult. It might even have been a pleasant surprise. But for the majority of newcomers to our churches, it is not the easiest thing they have ever done! It's not that Adventists are unfriendly people – quite the opposite. In fact it is very likely that your church, as with most Adventist churches, prides itself on being friendly and does everything it can to make visitors feel welcome. Unfortunately, being *friendly* is not necessarily the same thing as being *user-friendly*, as George Barna's definition of the term suggests:

'What does it mean for a church to be user-friendly? It

means providing people with an accessible way to worship
God, a comfortable place to bring their friends, and a sensi-
tive, creative community they can belong to – one that is wise
enough not to get in the way of the task at hand: reaching the
world for Christ.[2]

Being a user-friendly church is all about being sensitive to
the needs of those we serve, our church members as well as
our guests, so that we can be a help rather than a hindrance
on their spiritual journey. And that takes a great deal of grace
and wisdom, because different people have different needs.
It's true even in everyday life. For example, when some
people go into a shop to buy clothes, they love to have an
assistant standing by who is constantly making unsolicited
comments. You know the kind: 'You should try *this* jacket'.
Oh, yes, you look *excellent* in that suit' 'Really, blue is your
colour, etc.' I suppose it makes them feel important. But not
me. When I go shopping for clothes – or anything else for
that matter – that's the last thing I want. I'm one of those
people (the large majority, I think) who needs space. I need
peace and quiet and uninterrupted opportunity to see for
myself what's available, and at the same time know that
someone is there to answer my questions and provide help if
I need it.

Going to church, especially for the first time, is no different. Some people may appreci-
ate being given a flower and a
name badge and a personal
welcome from the platform,
plus a hug at the end of the
service, but that kind of treat-
ment would turn others away
for good. What they most

likely need is space, freedom to look around and see what's going on, and someone at a safe distance who can answer their questions if they have any.

But there's more to being a user-friendly church than that. A user-friendly church is primarily an outward-looking church, rather than an inward-looking one. It devotes itself to understanding the world around it and reaching those outside its membership, rather than serving its own needs. It is made up of people, whether new to faith or long-term members, who are more concerned with the comfort of the friends they invite to church than their own. It consists of Christians who simply don't fit the stereotypical image that, as one newspaper correspondent put it, *'Christians are a dim, ego-tripping minority which is dead set on telling everybody why they ought to become Christians, instead of finding out why they aren't.'*[3]

User-Friendly Principles

In his challenging book: *New Era, New Church,* Steve Chalke goes some way to addressing this issue by suggesting that British congregations which want to take their mission seriously in the twenty-first century must be able to offer certain assurances to unchurched people, if they are ever going to make an impact in their lives. Notice the titles of the ten chapters of the book:

- We will make you welcome
- We will be family-friendly
- We will make sure you can hear clearly
- We will be practical and relevant
- We will help you explore answers to your deepest questions
- We will offer you time to stop and think in a busy life
- We will help you make sense of the Bible and who Jesus is

- We will make sure your visit will be helpful and challenging
- We will help you discover for yourself God's Love, acceptance and forgiveness
- We will offer you the chance to make a new start

I list these points here without comment, and simply to illustrate what we're talking about. Look at the list and you will see that all the points have at least one thing in common: they are concerned with the questions, needs and comfort of people outside the church. They remind us of Archbishop William Temple's observation that *'the Church is the only society in the world which exists purely for the benefit of its non-members.'*[4]

Unfortunately, Chalke's choice of titles might also send the somewhat patronizing message that 'we (the church) already know all the questions/problems you are going to ask and have all the answers', which is precisely one of the reasons why unchurched people are 'turned-off' the church. As Christians we may well have what others are looking for, but our attitude must never be patronizing. Nevertheless, if my future church scored well on each of those ten points, I think we would be heading in the right direction.

Let's consider the broad principles, then, of what it means for a church to be user-friendly. If my future church is going to be truly user-friendly, it must qualify in four areas. First, it must be genuinely interested in people. Second, it must be culturally relevant while doctrinally pure. Third, it must be able to respond quickly to ministry needs and opportunities. Fourth, it must be comfortable with change. Let's consider those four qualities in more detail.

Some Practical Questions
for the User-Friendly Church

- Are the toilets clean (at 1pm as well as 9.30am)?*
- Does the church bulletin carry visitor-friendly information and is it well-produced?*
- Is the building comfortably warm and well ventilated?*
- Is the seating comfortable?
- Is the church tidy?
- Is there sufficient lighting?
- Can people sitting at the back hear as well as those at the front?
- Has provision been made for the hard of hearing?
- Is there wheelchair access to the church building and toilets?
- Are there distracting signs or posters in the place of worship?

*These are the three leading issues which determine visitors'
first impressions of a church

Genuinely interested in people

The good news is, being a user-friendly church is as simple as that. The bad news is that it's difficult, humanly speaking, for people to be genuinely interested in other people in the way Christ expects of them. People are naturally interested to know *about* other people, which explains why gossip and television soaps will always be popular. Interest *in* the well-being of others, however, especially if it is at the expense of our own, is not natural. As we all know only too well, human nature is essentially selfish.

'Genuine interest in people', therefore, cannot be an agenda item to be discussed, voted and accepted at a church board or business meeting. According to Scripture, genuine concern for others is the fruit of a living faith in God, the result of the Holy Spirit's activity in our lives.[5] (The shock-

172

ing truth is, according to Jesus' parable of the sheep and the goats, that it is also the only criterion used in the final judgement to distinguish the righteous from the unrighteous.[6]) But He can use us only to the extent that we are willing to be used.

'Genuine interest in people' is costly. It takes time, emotional and physical energy, and resources of all descriptions to demonstrate genuine concern for people, whether through the development of new friendships, or more formal ministry programmes. Here are a few things that carry a price tag:

Meeting people where they are. As we have already observed, this is what Jesus did. It wasn't a method of evangelism: it was His way of demonstrating His interest in them. Sometimes this meant being in a particular place at a particular time, as in the case of His night-time meeting with Nicodemus, who apparently was unwilling to talk with Him under any other circumstances. Sometimes it meant breaking local customs, as when He did the unthinkable and talked with the Samaritan woman at Jacob's well. Sometimes it meant risking His reputation, as He did when He made a regular practice of mixing with tax collectors and sinners. He took time to study Jewish law in order to understand and relate with the religious leaders of the day. He also kept up to date with current events and topics of ordinary conversation so that His teaching stories or parables would be meaningful to the common people.

In every case, Jesus had to put Himself out, stay out late, walk the extra mile, or in some way think and act outside the box of Jewish culture and tradition in which He had been brought up, and we should not think that was easy for Him just because He was the Son of God! But that was how He made friends and won hearts. That was why people, ordinary people, loved Him.

Jesus still meets people where they are

A young woman was sitting at a table in the corner of a nightclub a year or so ago, totally spaced out. It was 2 am; she was high on drugs, did not know what was going on. But that's how she preferred it – she'd broken every rule in the book, had no friends; her life was a mess. A new piece of music came on – a blasphemous piece of music. The devil was calling Jesus all the names under the sun. But the woman didn't hear the blasphemy. Through the noise and the beat and the flashing lights and the smoke, all she heard was the name of Jesus, over and over again. Something within her came alive. She suddenly realized what she was doing with her life. And even while the music was playing, she left the night club and phoned a pastor she chose at random from the *Yellow Pages*. Soon after, she started Bible studies, became a Christian, was baptized, and is now a member of one of our churches.

Paul understood this, and made it a principle of His own life and ministry: *'I make myself everybody's slave in order to win as many people as possible. While working with Jews, I live like a Jew . . . when working with Gentiles, I live like a Gentile . . . . Among the weak in faith I become weak like one of them . . . So I become all things to all men, that I may save some of them by whatever means are possible.'*[7]

What would it mean to apply the same principle to our own circumstances? Perhaps more than we might feel comfortable with. But maybe in the past we created barriers to friendship and ministry, because we were unwilling to pay the price. How can we 'meet people where they are', unless we are willing, at least occasionally, to meet them in their usual meeting place, i.e. the pub or bar. How can we understand people, if we do not visit their world by reading the newspapers they read, or watching (sometimes!) the television programmes they watch? How can we come close to people, unless we show an interest in their interests? Genuine interest in people cannot be demonstrated in a vacuum. It can be expressed only in the context of other interests or activities – *their* interests and activities.

Perhaps one of the best ways of meeting people where they are is to get involved in local community projects. As Adventists we tend to offer to our neighbourhoods services which duplicate what others are already doing (such as soup runs, youth clubs, etc.). In many cases, however, we would do better by supporting existing activities which desperately need more helpers. Duplicating community services simply for the purpose of having an Adventist own-brand of everything in town hardly helps us to meet people where they are.

Friendship. This chapter began with the statement that 'being friendly is not necessarily the same thing as being

user-friendly'. *If that is true,* it's also true that the user-friendly church will be friendly, and that the members of that church will take the subject of friendship very seriously. In fact, it would be impossible to be an active member of a user-friendly church and not be personally engaged in building friendships with people who don't go to church and/or have not yet come to faith in Christ. These days most conversions begin at the level of friendship, with no strings attached. And building that kind of friendship can be costly.

Friendship does not start on the doorstep of the church. If

175

we don't know how to relate in a user-friendly way from Sunday to Friday, how shall we manage on Sabbath? If we are not developing real friendships with unchurched people in the neighbourhood of our homes or our places of work, how on earth do we hope to succeed inside the four walls of a church building (or a scout hall, come to that, if that is where the church meets)?

Making friends takes time. Most of us are so busy we probably don't *have* time to cultivate new friendships. So if we are serious about this, we are going to have to *make* time. That means devoting time that we presently give to something else to building new friendships. And since time spent at work is non-negotiable, and time with our families is sacred and probably too little already, we may just find ourselves looking at the time we spend on church activities. As Mike Hill, an archdeacon in the church of England, observes:

'It may well be that if we are to become serious about evangelism, one of our starting points will be a review of our church activities in order to give time to our church members to develop relationships with non-Christians.'[8]

That may be a difficult thing to do for the congregation which has always made the church building and/or the pastor the centre of its activities. Since the time that most Adventists have available to devote to those activities is limited, asking them to take time to build relationships with non-Christians may mean that they may have to spend less time 'at church' in the traditional sense of the word. This in turn may mean that fewer traditional events can be continued with the same level of support as before.

For my future church the choice is simple. Either we take time to develop friendships with non-Christians which build trust and allow us the opportunity to share Christ in a meaningful way with them, or we continue as we are within the safety of our church-based programmes, out of touch and out of reach with the very people we are commissioned to share Jesus with. **Imagine the possibilities if each member was intentionally building friendships with three non-Christians.** Genuine friendship is the fertile field in which Gospel seed is planted most effectively, and Christian friendship is harvested most abundantly.

Tracts and Trust

One Sabbath afternoon we gave out 5,000 carefully designed leaflets to strangers we met on the street, inviting them to an evening programme at the church. Not one stranger came, and, to make matters worse, we found our precious leaflets in the rubbish bins which lined the road outside the church. On the other hand, our friends *did* attend, and we learned an important principle. Handbills and tracts have their place, but they work best when placed in the hands of friends.

Vulnerability. True friendship is based on trust; trust is based on honesty, and honesty sometimes makes us vulnerable. The culture in which we minister is 'post Christian', at least partly, because the church has too often pretended to be something it is not. People will not take us seriously – they will be suspicious of our offers of friendship and unresponsive to our parenting or marriage-enrichment seminars or other such community services, if they sense that we are not all that we claim to be. It's better to be authentic, to acknowledge from the start that we don't have it all together either as a church or as individuals, and run the risk of being misunderstood, than having to face the embarrassment of people discovering the truth about us for themselves. Jesus frequently made Himself vulnerable by His unpretentious life, even when it meant losing many of His followers (for

177

example see the narrative of John 6:25-71). He demonstrated, however, that vulnerability is a sign of strength, not weakness. It caused many to reject Him, but it enabled His true followers to accept Him. In the same way, genuine people today will 'open up' to us if we are willing to open up to them. Vulnerability is the door through which Christ comes to minister not only to, but through, His church. Scott Peck's observation is worth considering in this context:

'I am not advising anyone to be totally vulnerable, nor to be vulnerable at all times. Nonetheless, if you choose to be a healing presence in the world, it will be necessary to choose throughout your life to retain the capacity to be wounded to at least some degree . . . . If we are to be effective healers we must allow ourselves, within limits, to be continually wounded, and indeed, it is only out of our woundedness that we can heal or be healed.'[9]

Sensitivity. The other side of the vulnerability 'coin' is to be sensitive to where other people are in their lives. By being open about ourselves, we are inviting them to know us for who we are, but we should not expect them to respond immediately in the same way. Some people are much more reserved than others, and for all sorts of reasons. If self-disclosure is difficult for us, it is much more so for others. Everyone longs to love and be loved, to know and be known, but trust-based friendships which make such an experience possible take time to develop. We must be sensitive to the fact that this process takes much longer with some than with others.

We also need to exercise sensitivity in certain specific situations. For example, when we gather to study the Sabbath school lesson we should not presume that everyone knows the sixty-six books of the Bible and where to find them. Not everyone feels comfortable about reading or praying aloud. Not everyone is confident or competent enough to answer a theological question. Yet we want to involve everyone, especially our guests, in the class discussion. All can take part if we will take time to get to know them, and be sensitive to their needs and their limitations.

10 Things Visitors to Our Churches Need to Know

- Where do I sit?
- What books do I need?
- What facilities are there for my children and is there a place for pushchairs?
- Where are the toilets?
- What facilities are there for those with disabilities?
- Is an offering to be taken?
- How long will the service be?
- Is there a welcome pack which describes the church, its activities, and its involvement with the local community?
- Who is who?
- Is there anyone to talk to?

Clearly, different people need to be treated in different ways. It's true for our church members, but it's especially true for our guests. Members who are blessed with the gift of hospitality understand the need for sensitivity in the way we treat our guests, and while they should not be the only ones to greet visitors at the door, they should be the ones to care for them for the duration of their stay.

Creating a safe environment.[10] We have already addressed this briefly, but let's pursue it further. Why, after all, should the Holy Spirit create the desire in people to attend my future church if it is not a 'safe' place to be? If visitors are going to be confused, disappointed or hurt by what they see, hear or feel there, why should He direct them there in the first place? Consider three examples of what I mean – what *actually* happened in British Seventh-day Adventist churches not so long ago, and what *might* have happened if the churches and individuals responsible had understood what it means to create a safe environment for their guests.

Situation A

An excellent series of evangelistic meetings was being conducted in a well-located, newly-built town hall. Non-Adventist attendance was good, and the interest level was high. The evangelist had just presented the Bible's teaching about the Sabbath and invited his audience to attend the local church to experience Sabbath worship for themselves. At least a dozen guests arrived in time for Sabbath school, and all was going well until the time came to separate into classes. The teacher of one class stood up and announced, with a real challenge in his voice, 'Only those who have studied the Sabbath school lesson should attend this class.' It was more like a threat than an invitation, nothing like the warm welcome that had been extended to everyone at the beginning of the programme. Well, by the grace of God two or three non-Adventists survived the insult and eventually became members of the church. But the rest were never seen again. Can you blame them?

What might have happened? That over-zealous teacher and one or two members of his class could have been in the church foyer before the service, knowing that people who had never been to church before would very likely be attending. They could have been ready to offer assistance or information as necessary (this is not just the job of the official 'greeters'). Resisting the temptation to ask them to sign the visitors' book, they could have introduced themselves – as you do when you meet someone for the first time – and told them something about themselves. They could then perhaps have offered to sit with them, and, when class-time came, invited them to their own discussion group.

The class leader could then have led the study on a level that did not require a degree, using only the Bible, not the lesson quarterly, as the basis for discussion. The visitors really could have gained new insights from Scripture, seen how its teachings might apply to their own daily lives, and experienced the uniqueness of Christian fellowship, Christians growing together around the Word of God. Almost certainly, they would have wanted to return the following week.

Situation B

Once again, Sabbath school was involved. And that is not surprising. Sabbath school is probably more likely to be 'unsafe' for visitors than any other Sabbath meeting. At the same time it probably also has more potential than any other Sabbath activity for safely introducing visitors to the church family. But that wasn't the case in one of our churches last year. A husband and wife in their thirties, who had learned about the Sabbath through Bible study, decided to visit the local Adventist church, just to see what it was like. They had no church background, and they had only recently begun to read the Bible for themselves; so going to church for the first time was a courageous thing to do. They enjoyed the worship service. But, as they were leaving, a well-meaning elder gave them a Sabbath school quarterly, and told them they had to study it to be ready for the following Sabbath.

The following Sabbath came and went, but the visitors did not return. When someone called to find out why, he quickly learned the reason. That week's lesson was about stewardship, and dealt with the importance of a faithful tithe and abstinence from alcohol and tobacco. It was a case of too much too soon. They couldn't handle it. In fact, they could never see themselves living on that 'impossible level' of commitment. The Seventh-day Adventist church was not for them.

What might have happened? The well-meaning elder could have made himself more aware of the couple's background, and been more sensitive to their needs, realizing that that particular lesson quarterly was not appropriate for them. Either the church could have had an ongoing, user-friendly alternative to the Sabbath school lesson, such as a Christian parenting class or a basic Christianity series, or the Sabbath school class itself could have geared its discussion towards more general principles of stewardship, basing it on Bible stories or parables and informal personal testimonies of God's faithfulness instead of proof texts. The couple would have seen tithing and healthful living as 'relational truths,' i.e. not just true because the Bible says so, but because they work; they make a difference in the lives of ordinary people like themselves. That first Sabbath visit, instead of being a turn-off, could have been the beginning of a life-long adventure of faith and growth.

Situation C

Mary[11] attended church for the first time because her neighbour invited her. But it was also because she was worried. She was a single mother with a 10-year-old daughter. Life had always been a bit of a struggle, but nothing compared to this. A few weeks earlier a series of tests had confirmed that she had breast cancer. How would she deal with therapy? Would she see her daughter grow to maturity? Church seemed to be a good place to go in the circumstances. And it *was* good to begin with. Even her daughter was enjoying it, making new friends. There was just one main problem. It was a small church, and there were certain individuals who seemed to know everyone else's business, plus a bit more, if you know what I mean.

To all appearances, people were nice enough to one another, but conversation was superficial. After attending for several weeks, she realized that while she knew certain things *about* some of the members there – what they did for a living, how many children they had, where they went on holiday – she didn't actually *know* them any better than at the beginning. Worse still, it seemed they didn't really know one another either. Then one Sabbath in the foyer after divine service, she understood why. Accidentally she overheard the conversation of a small number of members huddled together in one corner. It was pure gossip about certain members not in the group, and it wasn't nice. The proverbial 'rumour mill' was in business in this church. If these Christians talked like this about one another, what were they saying about her behind her back?

Mary had been planning to share the trauma of therapy and her fear of the future with her neighbour and two or three others and ask them to pray for her. But she decided not to. Somehow she didn't trust them. A couple of weeks later she left the church, to walk that lonely valley by herself.

What might have happened? If real Christian community, which holds trust and accountability as sacred, had existed in this church – if those who shared confidential information from church committees with non-committee members had been called to account, and if gossip had been dealt with as the evil thing it is[12] – Mary would have found the supportive, genuinely caring community she needed. She would have discovered that valleys are densely populated places, perhaps even that she was not the only one facing an uncertain future; and in the open, trusting environment of a weekly small-group meeting, she would have found safety. Hopefully, she would have taken the ultimate step towards security and committed her life to Christ.

A 'safe' church environment – in which new Christians can take the first few steps in their new lives, and people seeking answers to their questions can feel at home – does not just happen. It takes more than prayer, although prayer would be a good place to begin.[13] It requires the education or re-education of church members, and a great deal of self-awareness. Tough love may have to deal with legalistic elements and judgmental attitudes. We must not expect new converts to run before they can walk. Young people must be able to talk about their spiritual growing pains, even if it makes the more mature saints among us uncomfortable. Their sense of security and safety in church is more important than our comfort. In my future church, and I hope in yours, one day such people will thank us for paying the high price of safety.

Culturally relevant while doctrinally pure

As everyone knows, Christianity is neither British nor American, African nor Indian in origin. Its origin is divine, not human. The Middle East was its cradle, but it was born in heaven. Through the incarnation of Christ, 'the Word made flesh', our transcendent God made it possible for mortals to know Him personally. In Jesus, God becomes relevant to us, and rather than compromising His status or reputation, His life on Earth had the opposite effect – He is now held in greater esteem than before. His willingness to humble Himself is His glory.[14] One day we shall see that the church's willingness to do the same is her glory, too, and far from compromising our beliefs or lifestyle, it can only serve to purify them, placing them in the only meaningful context there is – love for God, and love for our fellow man.[15]

What does it mean, then, for my future church to be culturally relevant? It means that my future church must do everything it can to enable people, wherever they are, to understand and embrace the life-changing message about Jesus in a way that is meaningful to them, without losing any essential part of that message.

A culture is basically the 'world' in which an individual or group lives. As everyone knows, teenagers live in a different world from that of their parents, but British teenagers also live in a world which is different from that of Sierra Leonean teenagers. How British teenagers think and experience life, how they interpret current events and communicate with the world around them, what is important and not important, is different from the way Sierra Leonean teenagers experience those things. A church that is culturally relevant presents the Good News in such a way that those who hear it can relate to it, understand the difference it can make to *their* lives, and accept it. It does more than that, however.

The need for cultural relevance does not cease at the point of conversion or baptism. As Leith Anderson explains, *'(Even) when modern pagans do become Christians, they may not be able to make the sociological jump to the traditional churches and organizations now available. They will need new forms and expressions of the church which are not now imagined – churches for the previously unchurched.*[16] So cultural relevance goes beyond 'meeting people where they are'. It means staying with them. Cultural relevance is important therefore, not just in the way we evangelize, but in the ongoing life of the church.[17]

How culturally relevant is your church? The fact that church membership is increasing substantially in some places must not be allowed to blind us to our actual effectiveness in communicating with the people who live within a stone's throw of the buildings where those growing congregations meet. As a well-known church leader observes, *'Churches that are growing numerically may still be of only marginal significance if they are not engaging with culture. The question "Why don't you go to church?" is about as meaningful as asking "Why don't you go to Mars?"'*[18] If numerical growth is coming from a small segment of the local population, the challenge remains for the church to learn how to engage with the culture of the majority who, for all practical purposes of communication, live on a different planet. And what about the youth growing up in our church? Is our inability or unwillingness to make the church culturally relevant to them one reason why so many have left?

Understanding misunderstandings. We might like to think that once people become Christians they become united or 'one' in Christ, but the reality is that Christian conversion does not make our cultural differences less significant than they were before. A person who has known only poverty is not suddenly able to understand the lifestyle and language of the rich and famous just because he has become a Christian. A Muslim family from the Far East who are accustomed to sitting on mats and rugs during worship do not suddenly feel a longing to sit on a pew or a chair the moment they declare that 'Jesus is Lord'. Nor should they be expected to.

At conversion our life-values change but our favourite musical instrument probably doesn't. In Christ we see all others as our equals, but we don't necessarily understand them any better. That's why any attempt to be culturally relevant to others who are different from ourselves is so often misunderstood and misrepresented. Even Handel was misunderstood and accused of compromising biblical truth when his *Messiah* was first performed.

'Handel's Messiah *is the most powerful oratorio ever written, and certainly one of the most popular. Every Christmas, millions of people hear the Old Testament prophecies of the coming Messiah and are moved by the Christmas story told in this great work.*

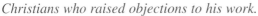

'Handel faced stiff opposition from sincere, thoughtful Christians who raised objections to his work.

'The criticism, which was to continue for nearly one hundred years, centred on the contention that Handel was profaning biblical truth – in other words, secularizing the sacred . . . . The message of the music was compromised, they claimed, by Handel's use of non-Christian musicians and soloists.'[19]

Who exactly were these Christian critics of Handel? One was a hymn writer by the name of John Newton, the famous slave-trader-turned-curate who wrote *'Amazing Grace'*. It's sad, really, since they were both trying to do the same thing. Both wanted to share Jesus with their contemporaries. Newton used one cultural format consisting of personal testimony with simple melody, suitable for congregational ministry. Handel used another in the form of a *'musically precise, intimate listening experience'*[20] designed for smaller groups of people (certainly not concert halls and large churches where his music is usually played today). If people like Handel and Newton had a problem with cultural relevance,

Worship music gets better with . . .

Practice. Musicians may not be professionals, but if given advance notice they can rehearse, although *not* on Sabbath morning before Sabbath school. An increasing number of churches rehearse the entire worship service on a mid-week evening.

Co-ordination. What a joy it is when every part of a worship service is connected around a central theme, and one part flows into another. Music should be chosen well in advance to make this possible.

Pre-recording. The music found in many hymn books, including the *SDA Hymnal*, is available on pre-recorded CD, and serves as a useful option for small churches which do not have a musician. Contemporary worship songs can be introduced in the same way.

Projection. Somehow the singing is better when the worshippers face a screen rather than look down into their hymn books. Following projected words on a screen is more user-friendly to the unchurched visitor than holding a strange black hymn book.

Hiring musicians. There are schools and colleges of music in many towns, and therefore many would-be professional musicians looking for opportunities to practise their skills. Such students, usually young, are often willing to serve as accompanists on a weekly basis for little or no charge.

Saying no, but saying it kindly, to those members who offer to accompany or lead singing or provide 'special music' who obviously cannot do it well however hard they try. The church at worship is not the time for worshippers and visitors to endure unnecessary pain.

misunderstanding one another's motives and methods, we should hardly be surprised if we have a similar problem today.

While on the subject of music . . . let's be aware that it now plays a much larger part in the way visitors evaluate our churches than it used to. On the one hand, it needs to be within the cultural mindset of the people we are trying to reach, and that includes the instruments we use and the people who lead the worship. On the other hand, it must be good, whatever kind of music we choose. The quality of our church's music is not determined only by the instruments that are used, but how they are played. It's not just the songs we sing, but how we sing them.

The 'Multicultural Church' is a term that is frequently used these days to describe what for some should be the ideal church in a multicultural society. This is the kind of church whose congregation is made up of several different nationalities. It is called multicultural simply because Africans, Asians and Europeans sit next to one another in church, use a common hymnbook, and are served by the same pastoral team. But is this really a 'multicultural church'? Not necessarily.

A church can be described as multicultural if the culture of the church reflects the cultural diversity of the congregation. In practical terms, this could only mean, among other things, that:

- Worship music (including instruments) will be varied, reflecting the tastes of the different people groups in the congregation.
- Worship services will be family-friendly, with equal appeal and interest for the different age groups.
- Preaching style will be varied. Some like it loud and demonstrative; others prefer it meditative and thought-provoking.

- Participation in church leadership and ministry will be representative of the various cultures, nationalities and social classes in the church.
- Language used in church will be language used and understood by long-term members and new believers alike. Bible versions used in preaching and teaching will be varied. Translation facilities will be available for those who find it difficult to understand English. Sign language or some other form of assistance will be available for the hard of hearing.
- Evangelistic style is varied to achieve the maximum response from the full spectrum of cultures represented in the target audience in the community.

It is obvious from this that being a multicultural church is not the easiest thing in the world. And it may not be the most desirable thing, either. It is true that a church should reflect the cultural mix of the society it serves, but attempting to do that through a single congregation may not always be the best way of meeting the challenge. It may be so busy trying to meet many cultural needs that it fails to meet any one cultural need satisfactorily. My future church could be more effective by adopting a different approach. Instead of attempting to meet the impossible challenge of being everything to everyone, it will recognize its limitations and specialize.

Different churches for different people. It's easy to mistake Christianity for culture. In the past, Western missionaries who carried the Gospel to foreign lands also carried their culture with them. As people became Christians in those foreign lands, they learned to sing western songs from western songbooks accompanied by western instruments, and attended church in western clothes. We now recognize that this was a mistake. Christianity must grow roots in the local culture if it is to have abundant local fruits.

The same principle applies to the modern world whose cities, especially in the west, have become home to people with widely-differing cultures. It is just as much a mistake for us to suppose (or insist) that one style of church will meet every cultural need and fulfil today's evangelistic challenge, as it was in days gone by. The need for different kinds of churches for different kinds of people is greater now than it has ever been. In the church, more than anywhere else, people should be able to celebrate their differences rather than lose them.

The all-embracing invitation that we include in our evangelistic advertising and place on the notice board outside the church, which says *'Everybody Welcome!'*, is almost certainly not as all-embracing as we would like it to be. Market research teaches us that the title of any given evangelistic programme will be attractive only to certain people, and automatically exclude everyone else. The colour, typeface and layout of the evangelistic handbill will likewise create a response from some but not from others. We know that the conventional design of a western-style church building with its spire or tower, however attractive and conducive to worship it may be to some, will be a distinct turn-off to those who need a more neutral, less 'religious' building to serve as their church base.

When we have issued our invitations, extended our welcome, and preached our message, we should not think that our work is finished. It has probably only just begun. If what we offer attracts only certain people, we have to learn why it does not attract others. Once we know that, we can choose between two alternatives. As a local congregation, we can:

Develop alternative approaches (as far as we are able) to evangelism and ministry which will attract and serve people who did not respond to our first approach, thus broadening the cultural spectrum within the church. For example, if our congregation consists primarily of elderly Christians, it will probably find that it mainly attracts other elderly people. If it wishes to attract young families, it will have to add a radically different ministry programme to its existing one. Even then, however, the chances of success are limited, either because its ability to do so is probably limited, or because the style of the new programme contrasts so much with the existing one that it creates an unacceptable level of discomfort for one group or the other.

Specialize. The reason the congregation in the above example wishes to attract young families is most likely that it wants to survive. After all, if most church members are elderly, the church itself is elderly, and its days are numbered, right? Wrong! The lack of young people in the church can be seen as a weakness, but it can also be seen as a strength. This church has a speciality. No one understands senior citizens as well as senior citizens do. So why should that congregation not build on its strength, accepting graciously the reality of what it cannot do, while accepting gratefully the reality of what it can do, and do it better than anyone else? There really is no need for that congregation to fear for its future. Through its specialized ministry to the elderly it can experience ongoing growth as it serves the elderly in its neighbourhood.

Obviously this is an extreme example of the specialized church, and I am not suggesting that every congregation with an ageing membership should be content to remain that way. But some recent experiments in developing culturally relevant churches for senior citizens suggest that the need is greater than we think, and that God can bless such initiatives.[21]

Consider other areas in which existing or new congregations might specialize:

Language/ethnicity. Most large towns and cities are host to many ethnic or language minority groups which are not served by existing Adventist churches. Some Adventist immigrants from such groups do attend them, but others, probably the majority, do not, and evangelistic programmes make virtually no impact at all. The large number of displaced immigrants in our cities is probably more open to the Gospel than the native population, but the only way immigrants will be reached in large numbers is through the specialized or targeted ministry of specialized churches.

Young families. One reason some families do not attend church is that the one or two churches they have tried either have a low tolerance level for children or their facilities for children and young people are poor or non-existent. Some congregations which have developed an expertise in family ministry and have invested heavily in meeting the needs of modern children are among the fastest-growing churches in the world, and actually attract worshippers from a wide age-range.[22]

Young adults. One unprecedented feature of the population that now fills many western cities and towns is that a large proportion are young adults without the responsibilities of children. Many under-30s have chosen to remain single (whereas in previous generations they would have been married and raising families). Many others are married but have chosen to remain childless or start families later in life. They identify neither with older folks nor with young families. Some such young adults have remained in our churches, but many have left (and will probably not return, unlike those young adults with families who tend to do so soon after their first child is born). This large group of people need churches which recognize and cater for their needs.[23]

Traditional/contemporary worship and ministry. It is difficult to be both traditional and contemporary and please everybody all the time. One reason why some people have stopped attending mainline churches is that they simply cannot tolerate the contemporary style those churches have adopted in recent years. There still is, and probably always will be, the need for churches which preserve the traditional forms of worship and ministry, and do it with excellence. However, most young people in our churches, and the majority of the under 50s who never attend church, live and express themselves in more contemporary ways, and need churches committed to excellence in contemporary church life and worship.[24] Developing such congregations is probably one of the most urgent challenges that we face as a denomination, especially in the Western World.

Unity in diversity, the biggest challenge? If responding to the ministry needs of the contemporary world is one of the most urgent challenges we face, some would argue that if we go down the road of developing different churches for different people, keeping the Adventist church united will become our greatest challenge.

So how can we diversify like this without compromising our unity as a world-wide movement? How can local congregations be encouraged to develop their own unique identities and still operate within a shared, global Adventist identity? Is there justification for the belief that this kind of specialization will lead to congregationalism and the disintegration of the denomination?

Perhaps we should remind ourselves that responding to the Gospel commission has always been a risky business, that following Christ has always involved a cross, that self-preservation results in self-destruction, and that the only way to keep our identity is not to hang on to it.[25] That is true not just of individuals, but also of organizations like ours.

My future church can and must diversify if it is to survive. How we might do so is the subject of the next chapter. Suffice it to say that there will be no threat to our unity if we:

* *recognize the difference between unity and uniformity.* According to Paul's analogy of the church as the body of Christ, it would be a disaster if we were all the same.[26] Our unity is in Christ, not the hymn book we use or the format of our services;

* *distinguish between Christianity and culture.* As we have already observed, it is normal to attach sacred significance to forms and ceremonies to which we have become accustomed over a period of time. But while Joseph Scriven's 'What a friend we have in Jesus', written in 1855, reflects a Christian truth that is universally meaningful, Charles Converse's melody of 1868 is a cultural expression of it and not universally meaningful. It can and should be sung in different ways to different music;

* *separate message and method.* The teachings of Jesus and the Advent message must never be compromised. But how we share that message must depend to a large extent on who we are and with whom we are sharing it. Christ's message was basically the same for all, but His methods of delivering it were as varied as His audiences.

Quick response to ministry opportunities

R. Hagebak has been quoted as saying that *'it is easier to ask for forgiveness than it is to get permission,'*[27] and that applies particularly to churches. Especially in well-established churches and institutions which operate by democratic vote and elected committees, it can be notoriously difficult to get the go-ahead to respond in new ways to new opportunities for ministry. But if we could ever afford to allow more than the absolute minimum amount of time to pass between identifying a need and responding to it, we can't afford it now. My future church must find ways to streamline its permission-giving process for at least four reasons:

1. Needs are greater. While this is an age of unparalleled prosperity and opportunity, it is also an age of unprecedented pain and suffering. World population is larger than ever before. The gap between the haves and have-nots is wider than ever before. Natural disasters, civil wars and other national tragedies are on the increase, as is the level of felt personal need in our own towns and cities. On the one hand materialism has raised our expectations of what life should be like; on the other hand it has lowered our tolerance-level of the pain we feel when those expectations are not realized. Whether the need is a devastating flood in Mozambique or loneliness in London, it is happening in the present, not the future. People cannot or should not be expected to wait for relief if we are in a position to provide it. My future church

196

must be able to identify new ministry needs and opportunities and respond to them as quickly as possible.

2. Needs-oriented evangelism is one of the eight key characteristics of growing churches world-wide.

As Christian Schwartz says:

'It is the task of each Christian to use his or her gifts to serve the non-Christians with whom they have a personal relationship and see to it that they hear the Gospel and come in contact with the local church. The key to church growth is for the local congregation to focus its evangelistic efforts on the questions and needs of non-Christians.'[28]

'Needs' may be physical, social, or spiritual. As Christians we must learn to scratch where people itch. All the evidence is that there is no shortage of a harvest out there. We just need to use the right reaping method. Over the past two or three decades we have observed a sharp decline in the effectiveness of our traditional public evangelistic approaches, yet new people continue to come to many of our churches.

Why is this? In most cases it's because individual members take a personal interest in visitors. If this is happening as the result of occasional, personal initiative, it could happen much more if we were intentional about it as a church, encouraging, facilitating, and empowering ministry initiatives, and not getting in the way by withholding or delaying permission for new and creative ministries.

3. Church members are more aware of their spiritual gifts. Thanks to what God has done among us in recent years, many believers know what their ministry gifts are, and want to use them. They should not be expected to limit their Christian service to projects decided at Conference or church board level. Rather, they should be encouraged to identify and respond to ministry needs and opportunities, inside or outside the church, that are compatible with their passions, gifts and personalities,[29] individually or in small, short-term ministry teams. So if church member Mary and four of her friends want to do something about a need in their church or neighbourhood which is not being met, they should be encouraged to begin that new ministry without having to wait for the approval of the Personal Ministries committee, the board of elders, the church board and the treasurer. By then it may be too late anyway.

Not so long ago, a group of Adventists proposed a plan to raise £50,000 for an overseas Ingathering project. The idea was good and the project was worthy; but they were given the red light because the timing was wrong and there was no means available to process the additional income. This top-down delaying of grass-roots initiatives should be replaced by a rapid permission-giving system, which cuts queuing time and encourages members to be responsive to Spirit-led opportunities.

4. Unnecessary delay is inexcusable. A few decades ago, methods of transportation and communication limited the flow of information and assistance. It was impossible to respond to needy situations faster than steamboats, second-class roads and inadequate telephone lines would allow. Now, however, if disaster strikes on the other side of the world, we probably hear about it more quickly than we know about the personal tragedy that happens on the other side of the street. We have up-to-the-minute news coverage not only of what is happening, but of what people are thinking, both at home and overseas. This is a fast-moving age in which rapid response is not only possible, but expected of us.

Streamlining the permission-giving process. What can we do to become more efficient in this area? William Easum, full-time church-growth consultant to religious organizations world-wide, maintains that a new mind-set, a new understanding of ministry, is needed before structural or organizational changes are attempted. (We may not agree with every suggestion that follows, but each could certainly provide the basis for some lively discussion!) Easum believes that this new, permission-giving mind-set should understand that:

- *'Freedom, grace and trust are more important than control and approval.'*
- *'Exercising spiritual gifts is more biblical and effective than representative democracy.'*
- *'Discernment of God's will for the Body of Christ is more the domain of individuals than committees. Permission-giving churches are more concerned about each person finding his or her distinct ministry and place within the Body than with the health of the Body. If each part is whole, the Body will be whole.'*
- *'Servanthood is more important than holding an office or sitting on a committee.'*
- *'Servants exercise their spiritual gifts because of a gratitude in their heart for what Jesus Christ has done in their lives.'*
- *'Ministry is understood to be helping people instead of running the church. Running the church and making decisions is ministry only for those who have the gift of discernment.'*
- *'Instead of church leaders asking people to fill pre-determined positions or programmes, individuals are asked, "What gifts do you bring to the body of Christ so that, if we equip you to use them, the Body of Christ will be more whole and so will you?"'*
- *'The laity do most of the pastoral ministries and taking care of one another, not the pastor.'*
- *'Instead of rotating from one church office to another*

199

throughout their lifetime, laity dig deep into one area of the church and they find someone to mentor as their replacement.'

⟐ *'Programmes develop from the bottom up and the side in, instead of from the top down.'[30]*

What do you think? Some of Easum's suggestions are radical, but most have a strong biblical basis; so think them through before you dismiss them out of hand. I certainly hope my future church will adopt this new mind-set for ministry. We can then look at the following practical steps we can take to streamline the way we identify and respond to ministry opportunities:

Develop vision, mission and value statements.[31] Together, these three statements (some organizations combine them in a single paragraph) give a clear, focused picture of what a church believes it is called by God to do. If they are already in place, now would be a good time to review them and refine them.

The vision statement is a summary description of what the congregation hopes to accomplish or become. It is more specific than the mission statement, providing the challenge to move from where it is (point A) to where it wants to be (point B). With mission and value statements in place, a congregation can build the ministry strategy that will enable it to move from point A to point B successfully.

The mission statement defines as specifically as possible what the church sees as its reason for existence, and provides a reference point for all future ministries. It keeps church leaders and teams on track. It should represent the mind of the congregation as a whole, and should be concise enough to be remembered, in principle if not word for word, by every church member.

The value statement sets out the principles that govern

the way ministry is done, and provides a circle of opportunity within which individuals and teams can live out the mission and vision of the church, without having to get permission for every detail of their chosen ministries.

Allow only functional structures to remain. Any department or activity that does not serve the mission of the church, however long it has been part of church life, should be laid peacefully to rest, rather than continuing to drain the church of resources that could be used more effectively elsewhere. In order for my future church (and yours) to be able to respond quickly to ministry opportunities, less time needs to be spent talking about mission, and more time spent doing it. We need a minimum of committees, involving a minimum number of people, to speed up rather than slow down the permission-giving process.

This may mean that the organizational structure of my future church will be different from that of your future church. Your congregation may be very much larger than mine, or our nurture and evangelistic ministries may differ because the people you serve have different needs from those of the people we serve, and our structure must be tailor-made to suit our requirements.

Encourage teamwork. *'Teamwork makes a dream work'*, so the saying goes, and it is true. Our present departmental framework is second to none, but without a sense of teamwork departments tend to be competitive, each trying to get as large  a slice of the resources cake as possible (which includes persuading church members to support their programmes). For the purpose of streamlining and efficiency, while my future church needs to reduce the number of its departments and committees to a minimum, it also needs to find a way where-by they can more effectively work together and support one another.[32]

The *'Church Ministries'* concept, proposed in the 1980s and never fully embraced, may still have something to offer us in this area if the principle could be applied to include all departments in the local church. One possible way of doing this might be to set up four co-ordinating committees:

- *The Steering Committee,* which gives 'permission' for new ministries, provides financial support, prevents duplication of effort, ensures organizational standards for accounting, and holds all other activities/teams accountable to the church's mission, vision and value statements.

- *The worship committee,* which co-ordinates all worship events including Sabbath school, although the Sabbath school has its own leader.

- *The Nurture and Evangelism Committee,* which co-ordinates the departments of Personal Ministries, Family Life, Community Services, Youth, and others as needed, each with its own leader.

- *The Buildings Committee,* which co-ordinates the care and operation of church property.

Instead of a traditional church board, a monthly church ministries meeting could bring the whole church together for fellowship and discussion of the overall life of the church. One congregation I know which does this has no nominating committee as such, but uses this monthly event as the opportunity for members to raise and respond to ministry needs.

Encourage the formation of ministry teams. Ministry teams are small groups of believers who share a common vision and a common burden for specific, often short-term, ministry needs. They are not appointed or given their job description by the church, but recognize a need and develop the strategy for meeting it themselves. They may be an already-existing holistic small group in the church, or a new group which comes together just to address a need and afterwards disbands. In one very large church I visited, there were over one hundred such specific ministry teams, including one made up of motor mechanics, whose ministry was to repair cars for people unable to pay for them! Several people have become Christians as a result of their labour of love.

One of the advantages of this system is that ministry teams are often able to be self-supporting. Their chosen ministries usually require the sacrifice of time more than money, and what money they do need they often raise themselves. It represents an approach to service which a growing number of non-Adventist churches are adopting, and which my future church would do well do take on board.

Comfortable with change

We began with the subject of change in the introduction to this book and as we approach the end of the book it must be mentioned again, because change is the order of the day. Make no mistake about it; just as today's world is totally different from yesterday's, so tomorrow's world will be totally different from today's. Yesterday's changes caught us by surprise. We didn't know how to handle them, and we were left behind. Let's not make the same mistake twice. We must get used to change, take advantage of change, live, if necessary, on the cutting edge of change.

God Himself is in the business of changing things, setting the stage for the return of His Son and our life-changing Lord. Some of us may yearn for 'the good old days', but our survival and success do not lie in doing what we've always done, but in keeping up with what God is doing. The changes we are seeing in the world around us are not all bad. More likely than not they are evidence of the creative hand of God preparing the way for the finishing of His work. The user-friendly remnant church of the twenty-first (and no doubt the last) century must not only be comfortable with change but highly value it if it really is to be His mouthpiece to *'every race, tribe, language and nation.'*[33]

For the sake of evangelism. Just as evangelism is the primary reason for the church's existence, so evangelism is the reason why we should be comfortable with change and make it work to the advantage of the Gospel. The best days for evangelism are still ahead, if we handle future change positively.

Unfortunately, our tendency to separate ourselves from anything associated with our 'before Christ' lives has resulted in our churches' being cut off from the very communities they are called to serve. In the past, this was not such a problem; people were more open to what Christians had to say and would respond to an invitation to attend public evangelistic meetings in large numbers. But times have changed and that no longer happens. If we want to look forward to a Pentecostal harvest from areas of society we have not touched before, we need to adopt a more user-friendly approach in our evangelism.

The table overleaf explains why a more relational, user-friendly approach is needed in the way we plan and conduct our evangelistic activities.

The New Paradigm of Network Evangelism[34]

Old Paradigm

Truth

Right was right; wrong was wrong; and truth was absolute. All we had to do was to prove the Sabbath was on Saturday, and an honest person would accept it. The main question we had to answer was, 'Is it true?'

Decision

Evangelism was an event aimed at gaining decisions.

Winning

The primary purpose of evangelism was to win converts.

Few

Evangelism was the work of a gifted minority. The work of the majority was to support them.

Evangelist

Evangelism happened where the evangelist was, usually in a public meeting.

New Paradigm

Relational Truth

Truth is only meaningful within re-lationships. As Jesus said, all Scripture finds meaning within the two great principles of love to God and love to our fellow man. The main question we now have to answer is, 'What difference will this make in my life?'

Process

Evangelism is a process beginning with the development of friendship and lasting long after baptism.

Keeping

Keeping converts in a growing experience with Christ is as impor-tant as winning them.

Many

Though not all have the gift of evan-gelism, all are ministers of Christ and can do evangelistic work as they are taught by those with the evangelistic gift.

Cell

Evangelism takes place primarily through the cell, as membersof the body work and witness together. Public sowing, growing and reaping events are organized to support the process.

Clearly, *friendship* will become increasingly important as the seed-bed of evangelism. *Door-to-door* work will be less 'preachy' or confrontational and more service oriented, possibly connected with prayer walking or some form of survey.

Public evangelism will probably remain as important as ever, but it will function differently. In Britain and Europe at least, very few secular people now attend intensive series of nightly doctrinal presentations over three to five weeks. Well-produced, once-weekly, ongoing, needs-based seeker-style services may prove to be a better way to go, especially if they are linked to an ongoing friendship or small-group ministry which helps provide the seeker audience.

Small groups will increase in importance, and many or most churches will see that making the transition to a fully operational small-group church model is the only way forward. One of the characteristics of our highly mechanized and mobile society is loneliness. According to a recent survey, one third of English people have not met their next-door neighbours, and those who know one another barely speak.[35] This is in a country which was once famous for its neighbourliness!

People's basic needs have not changed. We still need to live in community, for that is how God created us to function best. Small groups of Christians meeting regularly for worship, edification and witness can provide that community which people need so much. Evangelistically they can provide:

- a safe environment for people to explore the basics of the Christian faith before they are ready to attend church services or evangelistic meetings,
- ongoing nurture for new believers after baptism,
- opportunity for new believers to discover and use their spiritual gifts in ministry.

Unprecedented opportunity for the user-friendly church. From a Christian point of view, we could use various words to describe the time in which we are living, including breathtaking, disturbing, unsettling, difficult. But surely the bottom line is that it is a time of opportunity for the church, unparalleled by any previous period. It's such a privilege to be part of Christ's church now.

We have yet to see how all the wonders of the electronic revolution will work to the advantage of our mission. We don't have all the answers for reversing the trend of postmodern Western society away from faith in Christ, but we do know that it will happen, and that God is preparing us for it even now. We don't know how the Lord of the church will bring all its various strands together as one before His return, but we do know that there are millions of Christians outside our own denomination who share our hope and many of our beliefs, for Christ Himself promised: *'"There are other sheep which belong to me that are not in this sheepfold. I must bring them, too; they will listen to my voice, and they will become one flock with one shepherd."'* [36]

That's why my future church and yours must be user-friendly. It's all about keeping the church door open so it can happen, and happen soon.

---

[1] Steve Chalke, *New Era, New Church* (Great Britain: Harper Collins, 1999), page 15.

[2] George Barna, *User Friendly Churches* (Ventura, California: Regal Books), page 5.

[3] Australian journalist Max Harris, quoted in Chalke, xiii.

[4] Quoted by Rob Norman in *Christian Herald*, 29 January 2000, page 15.

[5] James 2:14-17; Galations 5:22; Acts 2:38.

[6] Matthew 25:31-46.

[7] 1 Corinthians 9:19-22.

[8] Mike Hill, *Reaching the Unchurched* (Amersham-on-the-Hill, England: Scripture Press, 1994), page 31.

[9] Scott Peck, *The Road Less Travelled and Beyond*, page 194.

[10] The church is addressing this issue with training materials such as *'Safety Zone'*, available through Advent Source.

[11] Name and other details have been changed slightly to protect identity.

[12] 2 Corinthians 12:20; Romans 1:28-32. Note: Gossip was just one of a salad of deadly fruits that was poisoning the spiritual life of the church at Corinth when Paul wrote his second letter to them. It is an activity which springs from 'corrupted minds' which do not have a 'true knowledge of God', and it is one of a dreadful list of evils including greed, vice, and murder which come under the judgement of God, and which the evil one uses to destroy not only society but God's new community of faith.

[13] See sample of the 'Friendship Card' designed by Pastor Hamilton Williams which can be used as a basis for prayer, in Appendix D.

[14] Philippians 2:7-11.

[15] Matthew 22:37-40.

[16] Anderson, page 134.

[17] For an interesting consideration of the existence of various cultural identities (as distinct from ethnic differences) within the church, see Caleb Rosado, *Adventist Review,* 27 April, 2000. Article: When We Disagree, pages 8-12.

[18] Stuart Murray, *Church Growth Digest*, Autumn 1999 (Moggerhanger, Beds, UK: British Church Growth Association) Article: Contemporary Trends and Their Implications for the Church, page 8.

[19] Douglas D. Webster, *Selling Jesus* (Illinois, USA: InterVarsity Press, 1992), pages 25, 26.

[20] ibid, page 26.

[21] See Rory Keegan, Paul Simmonds, Anne Hibbert, *Unchurched People Welcome Here* (Warwick, England: CPAS, 1995), pages 20-24. This is the story of how the weekly attendance at All Saints Church in Loughborough has grown to 300 through its 'Senior Service', a programme of outreach and ministry to reach and 're-church' people in their golden years. The four o'clock service is varied, geared to the interests of the sixty-plus, and lasts no longer than forty-five minutes.

[22] Leaders of the Willow Creek Community Church in Chicago, known worldwide for its outstanding success in leading young to middle-aged 'unchurched' people to faith, explained at their 1999 leadership conference in Birmingham, UK, that the excellence of their 'Promiseland' children's ministries plays a major part in parents' decisions to join the church.

[23] A survey presently being conducted in the UK towns of Epsom/Sutton suggests that many childless young adults would prefer to worship in a church with others like themselves, without the distractions of children.

[24] Merton Strommen, in *The Innovative Church* (Minneapolis, U.S.A.: Augsburg Fortress, 1997), page 134,135 says of such churches:

- They feature music that tends to have emotionally expressive melodies amply supported by instruments.
- Services are typically visitor-friendly, made simple and easy to follow.
- Informality is emphasized for the sake of good communication, a key objective in a contemporary service.

- Services feature revitalized preaching where a text is unfolded into application or where the sermon starts with the needs of listeners.
- Services involve many people . . . such as lay readers, singers and musicians, speakers, and persons who share their personal faith.

[25] Matthew 16:24, 25; John 12:25, 26.

[26] 1 Corinthians 12:12-20.

[27] In William M. Easum, *Sacred Cows Make Gourmet Burgers* (Nashville, U.S.A.: Abingdon Press, 1995), page 9.

[28] Schwartz, page 35.

[29] See Bruce Bugbee, *What You Do Best in the Body of Christ* (Grand Rapids, Michigan: Zondervan, 1995) for the best small book I know which deals with ministry determined not only by giftedness but also passion and personality. Excellent Adventist training materials based on Bugbee's work in the form of *Connections* are available from Advent Source.

[30] Easum, pages 67-69.

[31] For a sample of these statements and how to prepare them, see Appendix B.

[32] It is a characteristic of Christians (especially young people) in the Western World that individuals are reluctant to accept the responsibility of leadership, but are happy to work in teams.

[33] Revelation 14:6.

[34] Developed by Laurence Singlehurst, editor of *Cell Church UK* magazine.

[35] Reported in *The Sunday Times*, 5 March, 2000, page 13.

[36] John 10:16.

Chapter Ten

New Birth or New Baby

Developing existing churches and planting new ones

'"I am telling you the truth: no one can see the Kingdom of God unless he is born again."'[1]

After all is said and done, there's only one really important thing for us to remember about the true church – it is as divine as it is human. It is made up of men and women who are as extraordinary as they are ordinary. They started life like everyone else, but they have been 'born again', radically changed by Jesus. The change is so fundamental that they 'see' things which others are blind to and experience what unchanged people cannot experience. They can 'enter' the kingdom of God, not just at some future time, but now. For the kingdom of God is not only a future paradise. It's a present reality wherever the followers of Jesus meet together in His name. He is the King of the kingdom. He meets with them as He promised. The church is His body. And where He is, there the kingdom is also.

Like people, like church. I hesitate to apply the words of Jesus about the need for rebirth in this way, but I believe it is reasonable to suggest that what is true of individuals is also true of churches. Churches, like people, are 'born' with unique personalities. Unlike people, however, churches – and their personalities – tend to live on indefinitely, long after the members who made them what they are have passed from the scene. Even though different people sit on the seats and lead the services, there is a strong possibility that the personality of a church, the way it thinks, speaks and acts, belongs to a previous generation, and fails to reflect the *living* Christ and what He is trying to do in and through that church today.

Just as new wine needs new wineskins, Jesus our Emmanuel needs *new* churches to serve as His body. Every so often churches need to do more than make a few minor adjustments here and there. They actually need a new beginning, not just a 'revival.'[2]
They must be born again or renewed with each new generation to keep pace with the needs of the changing world around them. Alternatively or additionally, they may need to give birth to a new baby (for example, a new congregation) in order to survive and grow themselves.

What about *your* future church? Will it be a slight modification of your present church? Or will it take a new birth, a new beginning, to bring it out of the realm of dreams and visions, and into the world of reality? Who knows? But remember: just as birth and re-birth are the result of divine/human initiative, so church renewal is the same. It's the result of human co-operation with divine will and power. As congregations we need to be open and responsive to God's will, but we also need to understand the options and the part we might be called upon to play. As Carl George puts it: *'Our purpose is not to invent a future but rather to discover the future to which God is calling His people.*[3]

The purpose of this brief final chapter is not to insist that every church needs to be 're-born', or give birth to a new congregation, neither is it to explain exactly how a particular church can turn its dream into reality. It is simply to clarify the options, and also perhaps to excite our expectations by including a few examples of what God is doing through His church right now.

Option A: Renewing an existing congregation

Ambitious, growing churches are like ambitious, growing people. They live out their lives through a succession of valleys and mountains, with each mountain a little higher than the one before it. Actually we spend more time in valleys than we do climbing mountains. And that's no bad thing. Valleys are more fertile than mountains, and it's through the 'daily round and common task' of life in the valley that people and churches grow best. But we do need a goal. We're not meant to stay in the same valley all our lives. The sight and anticipation of the next mountain top keeps us moving.

There's nothing quite so spiritually invigorating as being part of a congregation which has just caught a new, shared vision of the next 'mission mountain' which God is calling it to climb. It is proud of its past and grateful to its founders, but it is suddenly more aware of the climb ahead than the valley behind. (I say 'suddenly' because it seems this is how it happens, just like a birth. It's a long time coming, but when it happens, it really happens! Vision is caught more than it is taught. It's the 'Ah-ha, now I see' experience, the moment when 'the penny drops'.)

Sadly for some churches, however, it is so long since they were on a mountain top or anywhere near one that the idea of going or growing again has long since disappeared from the agenda. For all practical purposes they have come to the end of the road. They are already into the decline that comes with old age and infirmity. Hooked up to a life-support machine of maintenance ministry, they are in survival mode, hanging on for dear life until the Second Coming. Is it too late to resurrect such churches?

The good news is that no congregation of believers, however small, need go beyond the point of no return and die.

Just as the 'born again' experience is available to everyone, regardless of age or circumstance, so the new birth experience is available to every church. Wherever your church may be in its spiritual journey at the moment, it *can* be renewed and revitalized.

Even if things are going reasonably well but you have the conviction that they could be much better, your church can rise to new heights of excellence. Exactly how that will happen, heaven only knows at the moment. But in order for it to happen, the following conditions apply:

a. Belief in the future. That's another way of saying 'belief in God', for He is Lord of the future even as He is Lord of the past. When Nicodemus asked how the miracle of rebirth happens, Jesus explained that while the miracle itself is the work of the Holy Spirit, our part is to believe, to trust that Jesus can and will give us life. So whoever you are in your local church, however insignificant you think your influence is, *believe* in the future of your church. Pray more about it, and share your optimism for the future with others. Together with others, prayerfully begin to dream dreams and see visions of your future church, just as the Bible says we can.[4] The mental picture of your future church, although not clear in every detail, provides the blueprint to build upon.

b. Holy discontent with the present. It's one thing to find fault with the church and do nothing yourself to make things better. That's being destructive. It's another thing entirely to be dissatisfied with the way things are, even when you are doing the best you can do. That's being constructive. It also suggests that God Himself is stirring you, and He is probably stirring others also. If enough church members become aware that God is trying to say something important to the church, major changes can take place. Whenever the Holy Spirit was in evidence in the early church, He rocked the boat one way or another.

c. Release of the past. We should not forget the achievements of the past, but we can't wind back the clock, and there is no point in wasting energy trying to recreate it. We really do live in a different world; so the goals and achievements of the past cannot serve to measure goals and achievements in the future. We should celebrate the past, but, as George Barna says it so well, *'The future is not won by reliving the past.'*[5]

d. Commitment. It probably took quite some time for your church to develop its present identity, and it isn't going to change overnight. The process of revitalizing a church needs more than a week of revival meetings. As we have seen, it probably needs changes in its structure, its activities, and, of course, its very thinking. Even setting up a network of small groups as a basis for its ministry will itself require training and involve trial and error over a year or two before the church gets it right. So it may be several years before a congregation can stand together on the next mountain peak of achievement, fully transitioned into a new, relevant, fully-functioning biblical community. And that requires commitment, especially on the part of the pastor and/or local leadership. One characteristic common to almost all successful 'turn-around' churches is a long-term pastor. In the present scheme of things, a revitalized church will not be the result of frequent changes of pastoral leadership.

e. Hard Work. As with living the Christian life, so with building a Christian congregation – no one ever said it was going to be easy.

*'"Church" is a "hard-hat" area – a **working environment** . . . churches will not grow unless local Christians commit themselves to concentrate on doing right things . . .*

*'One impression of Paul's complex cornfield/building site metaphor in 1 Corinthians 3 is inescapably that "church" growing/building involves **effort**. And that "church" is therefore no place for those who simply want to pick devotional flowers or play around with bricks.'[6]*

If we are serious about the Holy Spirit's giving our churches a new lease of life, we have to be prepared for the consequences: frequent meetings to grow and clarify the vision; market research to determine the needs of the community; training first for leaders, then for every member in ministry; development and application of a co-ordinated, ongoing plan of sowing, reaping and keeping approach to evangelism; more social events than most of us are used to; better-planned and presented worship services; clean and tidy places of worship; more visitation during anti-social hours; learning the new language and skill of relational Bible study, and a lot more besides. It's definitely not a nine-to-five proposition!

f. Thinking 'outside the box'. That means thinking about possibilities we have never considered before. It means questioning everything the church is doing and asking if there might be a better way of doing it. It means looking at what other churches are doing, to see if we can learn from them. It might even mean thinking the unthinkable, doing what we have never done before, but seeing it in an altogether new light. Almost everything Jesus did (especially on Sabbath) was 'outside the box' of traditional Jewish thinking, and many despised Him for it. But we love Him for it; and I think He would love it if we tried to emulate Him.

Some renewing churches. I use the term 'renewing' rather than 'renewed' because, at least among the churches with which I am personally familiar, I can think of numerous churches which have a vision for change and are at various places along the road, but I'm not aware of any that have actually 'arrived' at the place they want to be.

For example, several churches around the South England Conference are beginning to experience the benefits of biblically functioning small groups, but none as far as I know has yet become a small-group church. In a different area of ministry, over the last few years the *Advent Centre* in London has developed a more contemporary form of Sabbath worship, and is presently experimenting with the idea of having Bible study groups and Sabbath school classes after the worship service every week. There is no separate Sabbath school programme as such. Following a break after the worship service, members and visitors go directly to any one of a variety of study or discussion groups. This is not just a cosmetic change or a juggling of services, but an altering of priorities, acknowledging the presence of God first in worship, then responding through small-group interaction.

For more than a decade, **Newbold church** has been developing a more diversified approach to worship. If you visit there you can choose from three different worship services with three different worship styles, and if you ask around you will learn that many people who were not attending church before wouldn't miss it now. That goes for a number of adults as well as many students and young people. Newbold's model is used quite widely elsewhere in the Adventist world, and could be used much more widely in Britain. If your church is overcrowded, why not start an early morning worship service? Or what about a youth church in the place of the AYS meeting, empowering young people to create a youth-friendly worship service built around the needs of their non-Adventist friends?

A much smaller church that is 'in transition' is the congregation at **Harrow**. Like many small churches, Harrow church has developed a strong sense of community among its members, even though it has the use of its rented meeting place only on Sabbaths. In addition to this, however, it is intentional about reaching unchurched people. Members are enjoying a more contemporary and participatory approach to worship and learning to build a 'safe', seeker-sensitive atmosphere on Sabbath mornings. In addition, the church has created the **Heart Café**, which functions once or twice a month as a place where members can invite their non-Adventist/non-Christian friends on a regular basis. To begin with, just a handful of guests attended. Now, there are usually twenty or more. That's not just because the food is excellent and inexpensive. The **Heart Café** is a great place to be.

Another church I could mention for a different reason is the congregation at **Tottenham West Green** in north London. The noticeable thing about this church is its warm, friendly atmosphere and its willingness and ability to accept people, whoever they are, just as they are. Consequently, it's quite normal to find several strangers in church on Sabbath morning who have just dropped in without invitation to see what's happening. I said 'consequently'. Is there a connection? Are they being led there?

I say again, these and other churches are renewing but not yet renewed. They have a vision and they're working on it. They are beginning to see results, but they would be the first to acknowledge that they have a long way to go. After all, re-birth, like natural birth, is a whole-body experience. Renewing an existing congregation means involving *every* part of church life in growing towards to its full potential – the quality of its worship, the quality of its community, the effectiveness of its evangelism, the development of its spiritual gifts and its ministry through every-member, and so on. A renewed or re-born church, on the other hand, is not one that has reached its full potential in all these areas, any more than a baby is an adult. It is simply one that is fully and gloriously alive.

Option B: Planting a new congregation

According to Peter Roennfeldt, *'Church planting means starting new congregations for unreached people groups or in unentered areas or cities.'*[7] It began with the Gospel Commission itself, and the apostle Paul was the first full-time church-planting pioneer.

The Adventist church was of necessity a church-planting movement in the early days, but its rapid growth during the following few decades of its existence was due largely to the multiplication of new congregations rather than the development of existing ones. Salaried pastors, instead of being 'tied' to a maintenance ministry of existing churches, were more or less expected to plant new ones. As James White wrote of new or young pastors, *'In no way can a preacher so well prove himself as in entering new fields. . . . If he be successful in raising up churches, and establishing them, so that they bear good fruits, he gives to his brethren the best proofs that he is sent of the Lord.'*[8]

The president of the Seventh-day Adventist Church at the time, A. G. Daniells, was equally emphatic about the need for the *'forward movement'* of planting new churches, though for a different reason. He wrote:

'When we cease this forward movement work and begin to settle over our churches, to stay by them, and do their thinking and their praying and their work that is to be done, then our churches will begin to weaken, and to lose their life and spirit, and become paralyzed and fossilised and our work will be on a retreat.'[9]

Who will say he was mistaken?

Tithe for church planting. There is much discussion about the use of tithe these days. Many congregations feel, for instance, that all or part of it should be retained for the building up of the local church and the payment of its pastoral staff. So why *does* all the tithe go to the conference? According to Russell Burrill, *'Preachers were hired, not to preach to Adventists, but to reach new believers and start new churches.'* (Therefore) *'Churches sent their tithe to the conference to support the clergy who were raising up new* *churches, not to support local pastors.*[10] As we have already noted,[11] early Adventists actually regarded the pastoral role as a local lay position and not a 'clergy' position; so it is not surprising that the tithe was used in this way.

Our present system of tithing, then, has its roots in a church-planting movement, not the local church maintenance system with which we are now so familiar. We can hardly imagine a modern Adventist church without a paid pastor! Maybe it is time to return at least to some extent to the original plan, and invest a larger portion of our resources in a new, ambitious, church-planting initiative. The need for new congregations is at least as great now as it ever was.

The need for new babies. As we have seen already, quite apart from the fact that in most countries there are hundreds of towns and cities in which there is no Adventist church, in today's world we need different churches to reach different people. But there are other reasons why we should consider this option seriously. Church-planting research has consistently shown that:

- *it is the most efficient* and effective form of evangelism;
- *it brings new life* and vitality to the individuals and parent congregations involved. Contrary to fears and expectations, if a church 'gives up' some of its most gifted leaders to plant a new church, invariably new leadership emerges from within the remaining membership to bring a new lease of life to the existing church itself;
- *it is visionary.* It encourages new, creative approaches to ministry, because a newly-planted church has no traditions to overcome, except those in the minds of its founding members;
- *it serves to remind* the church at large of the real reason for its existence.

Somehow, we must find ways of releasing more pastors and lay members who have the necessary gifts from their present church involvement, and empower them through training and resourcing to begin the urgent work of planting new and different churches.

Some possibilities. We have already considered some of the different kinds of churches that are needed for the different kinds of people we are called to serve. We need ethnic minority churches, contemporary churches, and traditional churches, to name only three broad categories. But in this age of diversity and individuality, there is room for lots of variation within each. Obviously there is need for caution, but there is even greater need for creativity, and it is possible to enjoy creativity and diversity within our churches without losing any essential part of the Adventist message or lifestyle.

Actually, long before the beginning of this post-modern age, Ellen White was calling for such creativity on the evangelism and church-planting front, and warning off those who were critical of it. She writes to us as she wrote to them:

'Some of the methods used in this work will be different from the methods used in the past, but let no one, because of this, block the way by criticism. There is to be no unkind criticism, no pulling to pieces of another's work.'[12]

Let's consider, now, one or two exciting possibilities of how such new churches might be born. Clearly, establishing new congregations in new areas should continue wherever practicable, but there are other ways to go and grow also, as increasing numbers of churches are discovering.

A thriving Adventist church in **Brisbane**, Australia, for instance, began just a few years ago when a small nucleus of believers began looking for ways in which they could make a real difference to the quality of life in their part of the city. They were so successful in identifying and meeting certain 'felt needs' that the new church became a genuine community church. People saw it as 'their' church, even though they were not members of it. Today it has several hundred members, and literally thousands attend its weekly seminars or benefit from its community services. Because of certain of its programmes, the incidence of drug abuse and street crime in the city has significantly dropped. It has made such a difference that a neighbouring town has requested the Adventist leadership to start a similar church there also!

The Café Church, Copenhagen, is another interesting church-plant initiative. Designed by young adults for young adults, it was started three or four years ago in the basement of the central Adventist church there. It is called the Café Church because that is exactly what it is. The worship room is decorated like a café and furnished like a café. And, as in a café, there is food, which 'waiters' serve in informal style. Young Adventists sit with their friends around tables, listening to contemporary live music, joining in worship songs, hearing the message preached, and discussing the issues raised.

As with most initiatives, this one began small, with a small number of Adventists inviting a small number of friends. Today, they have outgrown their meeting place and are looking for alternative accommodation. And, yes, they have seen some of their friends baptized. The Café Church is not everybody's idea of church, but it certainly meets certain young people where they are and satisfies their spiritual needs. It began as an experiment; the leadership team have learned a lot; and they are still working through certain issues and challenges. But that is what discipleship is all about, growing as you go.

Leamington Spa Mission is a bit closer to home, in more ways than one: it's British, and it has been a home away from home for many young people, some of whom have regularly travelled long distances just to attend every Sabbath. It began in 1991 with eighteen members meeting in a hospital chapel. Today it has a membership of over sixty, and a weekly attendance in excess of that number.

The initial 'target' group for growth was isolated and lapsed Adventists. The pastor, Allan Conroy, explains that it was important to take *'careful note of what people enjoyed, why they came, what blessed them most, and this helped a great deal in formulating worship styles that met the needs of the indigenous people. For some, myself included, we had lost our indigenous roots because we had been a part of other kinds of worship for so long. This was a fascinating self-discovery journey.'* Many Adventists in the multicultural environment of this and other countries can identify with his experience, especially if they are living away from home.

The church is now developing a seeker-friendly style of worship and church life and targeting the unchurched people who live locally. Several individuals have been added to the church through baptism, but plans for a larger harvest are being developed for the future. The main reason I mention Leamington Spa Mission here is because it demonstrates what a new church can do not just for its community but for its members. Still a largely commuter church, it attracts individuals and families from a very wide area, most of whom had little or no involvement with their church before.

Right from the start everyone was given equal opportunity to be involved in the decision-making process through regular business meetings, and even now there is no 'church board'. The serving of meals after Sabbath services and a full social calendar helped build relationships. When a building became available for purchase, everyone was involved through sacrificial giving and by helping with the extensive renovation work. For five years, twenty-five members or so were working ten to twelve hours every Sunday to make the building usable. Now they have their church home, and we pray that the best days for Leamington Spa are just around the corner.

Everywhere, it seems, Adventists are sharing the vision of planting new churches. Since the beginning of the annual 'Seeds' church-planting conferences at Andrew University in 1996, there has been a major escalation in new church planting initiatives, both by full-time pastors and by lay men and women (such as Rod and Donna Willey who started a new church in their dental practice surgery five years ago!). Ethnic minority churches of all descriptions are continuing to increase around the world. Even in countries where the progress of the church has been slow for decades, church planting is bringing a new lease of life. In Greece, for example, church planting has been made a priority throughout the country over the past three years, and approximately twelve new churches have been started. Now, that mission field is beginning to reap the benefits: whereas two or three baptisms were the annual average, over seventy converts have been added to the membership during that period. Is God opening the way for His church world-wide? I believe so.

Churches reproducing churches

Whether your present church is a new church or an 'old' church, whether it is restless with youthful energy and anxious to move forward or feeling its age and struggling with the challenge of change, why not start talking now about the possibility of 'having a baby'? The very idea might make some people laugh, as it did old Sarah who believed quite rightly that she was well past child-bearing age. But the question remains, *'Is anything too hard for the Lord?'*[13] For the young, growing congregation, the challenge of looking ahead and adding to the family two or three years down the line may be the very challenge it needs to keep it focused outwards, and save it from the downward spiral that so often follows the first five years of a new church's life. Similarly, it may be just what is needed for the church that has already served three or four generations of believers, has an ageing congregation, or has simply ceased to grow as it once did.

Imagine the possibilities if *every* Seventh-day Adventist church could give birth to another Seventh-day Adventist church within, say, the next ten years, if time should last that long! Imagine the possibilities if, by the life-giving power of the Holy Spirit, the old Adventist idea of churches reproducing churches was to be written into our spiritual DNA; so that as soon as a new church was planted it would itself set about planting another church, with its own unique character and mission.

We're not talking about multiplying churches here for the sake of it – we're talking about multiplying churches for the sake of the Gospel. We're not talking about doing something new – we're talking about getting back to our New Testament roots and doing what the early church did. And, of course, we're not talking here about every congregation having two hundred members with its own choir, church building and school – we're talking here about all sorts of different churches, some sharing a church building, others renting a school hall or community centre, others in their first year or two meeting in homes, and others . . . Well, who knows?

Who knows what any new baby will be like? Who knows what any baby will do when he or she grows up? No one, I suppose. Except, of course, we know that what usually happens is that young adults meet other young adults; they fall in love, get married and, hey presto, before you know it you have more babies. More people. It's what you get with a love affair. And that brings us full circle to where we started.

---

[1] John 3:3.

[2] The scheduling of regular 'revivals' in the local church calendar suggests that the church is in a constant state of dying. Re-birth and maintaining optimum church health could be the way to deep-seated, lasting revival.

[3] Carl George: *The Coming Church Revolution* (Michigan, U.S.A.: Fleming H. Revell, 1995), page 15.

[4] Joel 2:28, 29.

[5] George Barna, *Turn-Around Churches* (California, U.S.A.:Regal Books, 1993), page 48.

[6] John Bayes: Natural Church Development supplement in *Church Growth Digest,* Autumn 1999 Moggerhanger, Beds, UK: British Church Growth Association.

[7] Peter Roennfeldt, *Church Planting* (document produced by the Trans European Division, 1999), see preface.

[8] Quoted by Ron Gladden: 'Evangelism and Church Planting', *Ministry*, October 1999 (Nampa, U.S.A.: Pacific Press), page 6.

[9] ibid.

[10] Burrill, 50, 51.

[11] Page 159.

[12] Ellen G. White, *Testimonies for the Church,* vol. 7, page 25.

[13] Genesis 18:12, 14.

The Future Is Out There

The view beyond tomorrow

'And I heard every creature in heaven, on earth, in the world below, and in the sea – all living beings in the universe – and they were singing: "To him who sits on the throne and to the Lamb, be praise and honour, glory and might, for ever and ever!"'[1]

W ho knows what my future church will look like, or yours for that matter? After all, when will 'the future' end, and where will it lead? As we have tried to see our future church in our mind's eye, we have seen it against the backdrop of what we are familiar with, and by God's grace these dreams will become a reality. But that is by no means the end of the story, as you well know. For there will come a time, probably sooner than we think, when the backdrop will change, and much of what we are familiar with will change. Gradually or suddenly, attitudes will change, and countless individuals who once felt no need of Jesus will turn to Him, and will become His most able witnesses. Church buildings, which we have worked so hard to establish, will be totally inadequate. Institutions which have served the cause so well will have served their purpose.

As change follows change and Earth's final events follow one after the other with ever-increasing speed, most of what

227

is familiar to us now, perhaps even the structure and organization of our church as we know it, will give way to the one essential element of all our future churches – people. Not just any people, of course, but fully committed disciples of Christ, men and women and boys and girls who *'keep the commandments of God, and the faith of Jesus.'*[2]

My future church will probably have a slightly different agenda then to what it has now. Now we look to the future in anticipation of what will be and how far we still have to go. Then we will look back and marvel over what was and how far we have come. When Jesus returns to Earth to take His church-bride home; when we meet in small groups for Bible study and worship in those city mansions and quiet country cottages; when we gather around the throne every Sabbath for celebration, we will be overwhelmed, again and again, with the miracle of God's grace that has brought us from where we were to where we are. Once we were the church militant, then we will be the church triumphant. Over and over again, our thought will be, 'How can we thank Him enough for the privilege of being part of His church?'

Because, as we observed at the beginning of this book, the church really is an extraordinary, marvellous thing! Made up of ordinary people like you and me, it is very, very human. But as the body of Christ, it is wonderfully divine. So what *can* be said about this divine-human miracle except that it will always fall short of what it could be, and that it can always become more than it is? Even in the earth made new! Even for the rest of eternity!

And that is why I find the thought of my future church so exciting. God is infinite. There is no limit to His love and, therefore, no limit to our understanding and experience of it. There will always be room for growth and need for change.

What we do here and now until Jesus comes is just the beginning. After that, there will be no end.

That's why this last chapter is so short, because in the long term – in terms of eternity – I have no idea what my future church will be like. I just want to be there and grow with it. As for your future church, even in the short term, I have no idea what that will be like either. That's for you and your church to decide, and I hope that after reading these pages you will begin filling in the details and adding to this chapter without delay. And let's look forward to the time when *your* church and *my* church become *our* church, and we are all one in Him with the countless millions who will one day make up *His future church.*

---

[1] Revelation 5:13.
[2] Revelation 14:12, KJV.

Appendix A

The Worship Committee

A. Role of the Worship Committee

The role of the worship committee is to enhance the experience of congregational worship by careful planning and co-ordination of the worship programme. For the purpose of the suggestions which follow, the worship programme is understood to mean the weekly Sabbath worship service or 'divine service,' although an increasing number of churches are coming to recognize the value of integrating divine service and Sabbath school into a single worship event.

Developing the worship experience in a local church to its full potential involves:

- Long-term planning
- Medium-term planning
- Short-term planning
- Evaluation

1. Long-term Planning

Worship is very much a spontaneous, heartfelt response to the work of God in our lives. Nevertheless, to meet the needs of many different people, careful thought must be given to ensure that over a period of time the service of worship is sufficiently varied to meet different needs and provide an adequate and balanced worship 'diet'.

In many churches such long-term planning is done by the pastor alone, or the pastor and board of elders. The worship committee can help in this process, however, by:

- identifying the felt needs of the congregation;
- suggesting quarterly or monthly themes and individual sermon topics to ensure a certain flow or progression of experience from one worship experience to another;
- bringing creativity to the planning of special worship events such as baptisms, dedications, ordinations, flower and music festivals, and Christmas and Easter;
- assisting in the appointment of speakers and worship leaders.

Such long-term planning should be done during quarterly meetings of the worship committee called specifically for the purpose. The ideal is to ensure that the broad outline for a given quarter (including monthly/quarterly theme and speakers) is in place at least a quarter beforehand.

2. Medium-term Planning

During the first part of the weekly meeting of the worship committee, attention should be given to the worship service which will take place a month or so from that time. This is the opportunity to decide the following:

♦ **The content of the worship service,** based on the subject which has been chosen, and a clear statement of purpose, i.e. what the service is intended to achieve in terms of congregational response. This is the time to determine approximately how much time will be given to singing, special music, prayer, preaching, children's feature, drama, etc.

A possible outline of the service can be drawn up at this time, showing how each part of the programme might relate to every other part and contribute to the effectiveness of the whole. Suggestions should also be made as to who should present the various items listed above.

♦ **The style of the worship service.** This is determined to some extent by the subject and content of the service, but also by the worship participants, both presenters (their abilities, personalities and resources) and members of the congregation (what enables them to share most effectively in the worship experience). If the church is committed to making the Sabbath worship event meaningful to non-Adventist or non-Christians visitors, the choice of style is especially important.

Variety of worship style is important for many reasons. It prevents the worship event from becoming routine and predictable, keeps the worship experience fresh, and maximizes congregational participation and involvement. The following questions may help to determine the worship style for any given Sabbath:

♦ Is the topic for the day most suitable for meditation, celebration, or a combination of both?

♦ If there is an extended period of worship in song, testimony and prayer, should it begin 'high' (in praise) and end 'low' (in reflection) or begin low and end high?

♦ Will the speaker mainly teach or preach?

♦ What level of participation and interaction will best suit the topic and content?

♦ Should there be a platform party or should the presenters sit at the front of the church and only appear on the platform to present their individual parts?

♦ **Special features for the worship service.** Creative worship often needs visual, audio or other aids for maximum impact. Platform backdrops, flowers, and illustrative material for the sermon should be considered here to ensure that everything is available in good time. Special lighting, projectors, etc, should also be specified if needed.

3. Short-term planning
One half to two thirds of the weekly worship committee meeting should be

devoted to the detailed planning of the worship event a few days (five to seven days is ideal) before it takes place. All those taking part know by the end of the meeting:

- the precise order of service, how each part flows from the part before it and into the part which follows, contributing to the service theme;
- who does what and how;
- how much time should be taken for each part of the service, in order to keep roughly within the time period agreed for the worship service as a whole (especially important for visitors);
- which songs and hymns will be used. If a worship team leads the singing, vocalists and instrumentalists must know exactly how one song will lead to another, who will introduce items, etc;
- if there is a platform party, how many chairs are needed;
- how many microphones are needed and where they should be placed;
- what information needs to be made available verbally and/or via the church bulletin so that visitors can follow the order of service.

After these details are finalized, some churches go one step further and rehearse the entire service, including the sermon, in the sanctuary shortly before the actual event. You may not feel this is necessary in your church, but a certain amount of rehearsal is appropriate, especially for the worship-leading team (vocalists and instrumentalists) and other presenters who may lack confidence.

4. Evaluation. One of the most valuable exercises of the worship committee is the weekly evaluation of the most recent worship service. Asking 'How did it go?' or 'What did we do well and what could we have done better?' need only take five or ten minutes of the weekly worship committee meeting, but it's the best way to make sure that the worship we bring to God is the best we can offer.

B. Membership of the Worship Committee
There are no hard and fast rules on this one. One model which has worked well is to have a small worship committee core comprised of suitably gifted individuals who can provide continuity as regular members, who then meet with the individuals who actually present the items in a given worship service. Attendance at a typical worship committee meeting might look like this:

Regular Core Members	Additional Members
Church pastor	Speaker (if not the pastor)
A church elder	Worship leaders' representative
Music co-ordinator	Pianist, organist, or other musician
Two or three other gifted members	Children's feature presenter
	Other special participants

Appendix B

Vision, Mission and Value Statements[1]

A. The Vision Statement
Example:
To grow a Seventh-day Adventist Church that has a passion to reach lost Aussies and is a safe place for them to find Christ and grow to Christian maturity, because it is committed to being culturally relevant while at the same time maintaining and upholding the principles of Christ and His church.

Preparing the Vision Statement
What does God want us to do? Do not think of an extension of the present – but pray that the Spirit of God will develop a vision of what God wants ten years from now, for *'where there is no vision, the people perish.'* *Proverbs 29:18.*

When the Holy Spirit possesses our lives He gives vision. God has promised, *'"I will pour out my Spirit on all people. Your sons and daughters will prophesy, your old men will dream dreams, your young men will see visions."' Joel 2:28.*

Prepare your vision statement by responding to the following questions:
Pray that the Holy Spirit will give you a VISION of your church in ten years.

1. I think the single most important thing God wants our church to do is

   _____

   _____

   _____

   _____

2. If God would not let me fail, I think the most important thing God wants me to do is

   _____

   _____

   _____

   _____

3. Imagine you are a journalist preparing a report or documentary on your church ten years from now. Pray about the possibilities. What would you like to be reporting?

1. **What is the impact of your church in the community?**

   _____

2. **How would you describe the attitudes of people in your church?**

   _____

3. **How are members cared for and involved in mnistry?**
   What is the place of small groups for fellowship, Bible reading and nurture?

   _____

   Are members ministering according to their spiritual gifts?

   _____

4. **The Holy Spirit always brings growth:**

   a. How are members being discipled?

   _____

   b. How are unreached people groups being reached by Christians?

   _____

   c. Are lost people coming to know Jesus – and are new churches being planted? How many worshippers can you picture at your church?

   _____

5. **What type of worship experiences can you picture? To achieve your vision, would there need to be more than one worship service each week – and what forms might they take?**

6. **What type and style of buildings would be part of your vision?**

B. The Mission Statement
Example:
This mission statement is based on the acrostic G R O W

Glorify
Refine
Offer service
Witness

We will exist. . .
'To grow a people for God who:
Glorify Him in worship, are
Refined by His Spirit,
Offer their lives in service and are committed to
Witness the love of Jesus to lost Aussies.'

This Mission Statement will be popularized in the following way:
'A growing church, for growing people'

Preparing the Mission Statement
A good mission statement will be: (1) biblical, (2) specific, and (3) clear.
Prepare your mission statement by responding to the following questions:

1. Be biblical: What does God expect us to do?

2. Be specific: Why Does Your Church Exist?

   a. What would be lost if your church ceased to exist?

   _____

   b. How does your church differ from others? What are your distinctives?

   _____

   c. What does God expect your church to do? What business are you in?

   _____

   d. What is your church's single most important task?

   _____

3. Be clear: A good mission statement is easy to remember and communicate.

   a. Write out all you think needs to be said. (Then edit out the unnecessary words.)

   _____

   b. Summarize your answers in a sentence:

   _____

c. Does your mission statement incorporate the biblical purposes for the Church?

_____

C. The Values Statement

Example:

Core values are the building principles you hold that determine how you act. The best measurement of values is our behaviour. Below I have articulated the guiding principles important to me and which I seek to emulate. They are also the core values upon which I would base the new church.

1. PRAYER IS NORMATIVE: Authentic leadership and strong churches begin with and are sustained by 'a movement of prayer'. Full devotion to God is normative, NOT optional.

2. RELATIONSHIP BUILDING: God desires His church to restore relationships (to be repairers of the breach) and to build bridges for lost people to come into His kingdom. This demands love, acceptance, honesty, integrity, open communication and above all forgiveness.

3. TRAINING FOR MINISTRY: All are valued, each with a ministry to perform as they are trained, equipped and mobilized to exercise their talents and spiritual gifts.

4. SMALL CARE GROUPS: Small groups form the basis for growth as they can effectively reach into the community and provide a safe place for healing and growth.

5. GROWTH: Growth is a sign of life and depends on food. Spiritual growth depends on Bible study, prayer and sharing, which produces worship and service.

6. RELEVANT WORSHIP: Man's response to a gracious God. Worship must be worthy of God, up-building to man and culturally relevant.

7. BIBLE BASE: The Bible is the basis for truth, truth is eternal, our understanding is ever growing, and the way truth is communicated is ever changing according to cultural context.

8. FAMILY: Family is the basic unit of society as God designed it and therefore of the Church. Programming and structure must reflect this fact.

9. CHURCHES MUST REPRODUCE: The church exists to grow and reproduce growing more and better Christians and more and better churches.

236

10. WE GIVE THE BEST TO GOD: We must always offer the best to God.

Preparing the Values Statement
Prepare your value statement by responding to the following questions:

1. What do you look for and expect from people at your church?

   _____

2. How could your church be more Christian in its activities?

   _____

3. What attitudes and values do you think are the most important to those who participate in decision making, the ministries and activities (outreach, worship, etc) in your church?

   a. _____

   b. _____

   c. _____

   d. _____

   e. _____

   f. _____

   g. _____

   h. _____

4. Define what you see as the three most important attitudes in terms of how your church operates.

   _____

---

[1] Examples prepared by Pastor Ken Houliston as part of his proposal for the planting of the Southside Adventist Church in Brisbane, South Queensland Conference, Australia. Proceedure for developing these statements prepared by Peter Roennfeldt and used with permission.

Bibliography

Anderson, Leith. *Dying For Change*. Minneapolis, USA: Bethany House Publishers, 1998.

Arnold, Jeffrey. *The Big Book on Small Groups*. Illinois: InterVarsity Press Downers Grove, 60515, 1992.

Barna, George. *The Second Coming of the Church*. Nashville Tennessee, USA: Word Publishing, 1998.

_____ . *Marketing the Church*. USA: Navpress, 1993.

_____ . *Turn Around Churches*. Ventura, California, USA: Regal Books, 1993.

_____ . *User Friendly Churches*. Ventura, California, USA: Regal Books, 1991.

Baumgartner, Erich W. *Re-Visioning Adventist Mission in Europe*: Michigan, USA: Andrews University Press, 1998.

Beckham, Bill. *The Two-Winged Church Will Fly*. Houston, Texas, USA: Touch Outreach Ministries, Inc.

Beckham, William A. *The Second Reformation: Reshaping the Church for the 21st Century*. Houston, USA: Touch Publications, 1995.

Bilezikian, Gilbert. Community 101: *Reclaiming the Local Church as Community of Oneness*. Michigan, USA: Zondervan Publishing House, 1997.

Brierly, Peter, *'Christian' England: What the English Church Census Reveals*. London: MARC Europe, 1991.

_____ . *Act on the Facts*: London: MARC Europe, 1992.

Bugbee, Bruce. *What You Do Best in the Body of Christ*. Michigan, USA: Zondervan Publishing House, Grand Rapids, 1995.

Burrill, Russell. *Radical Disciples for Revolutionary Churches*, California, USA: Hart Research Centre, 1996.

_____ . *Rekindling A Lost Passion: Recreating a Church Planting Movement*. USA: Hart Research Centre, 1999.

_____ . *Revolution in the Churches: Unleashing the Awesome Power of Lay Ministry*. California, USA: Hart Research Centre, 1993.

_____ . *Recovering an Adventist Approach to the Life and Mission of the Local Church*. California, USA: Hart Research Centre, 1998.

_____ . *The Revolutionized Church of the 21st Century: The*

Explosive Power of a Church Built on Relationships. California, USA: Hart Research Centre, 1997.

Carey, George. *Planting New Churches.* Guildford, Surrey, Great Britain: Eagle (undated).

Cerna, Miguel Angel. *The Power Of Small Groups In The Church.* California, USA: El Camino Publishing, Newbury Park, 1991.

Chalke, Steve. *Evangelism Made Slightly Less Difficult.* England: Inter-Varsity Press, 1997.

Chalke, Steve with Radford, Sue: *New Era, New Church.* Great Britain: Harper Collins, 1999.

Cho, Paul Yonggi. *Successful Home Cell Groups.* New Jersey, USA: Bridge Publishing, Inc., 1981.

Comiskey, Joel. *Home Cell Group Explosion*: Houston, Texas, USA: Touch Publications, 1998.

Cox, David. *Think Big Think Small Groups.* Grantham, England: Stanborough Press, 1998.

Crabb, Larry Dr. *Real Change is Possible* – Inside Out. UK: Alpha, 1998.

Day, Dan. *A Guide to Marketing Adventism.* Boise, Idaho: Pacific Press Publishing Association, 1990.

Dudley, Roger L & Cummings, Jr. Des. *Adventures in Church Growth.* Hagerstown, USA: Review and Herald Publishing Association, 1983.

Easum, William M. *Sacred Cows Make Gourmet Burgers.* Nashville, TN. USA: Abingdon Press, 1995.

_____ . *Dancing with Dinosaurs Ministry in a Hostile and Hurting World.* TN. USA: Abingdon Press, Nashville, 1993.

Evans, Larry R. *From Cell to Celebration.* Orgeon, USA: The Neighbourhood Home Bible Study, 1998.

Finell, David. *Life in His Body.* USA: Touch Publications, Inc., 1995.

Finnell, David. *A Simple Guide to Active Cell Life.* Houston, Texas: USA TOUCH Outreach Ministries 1995.

Finney, John. *The Well Church Book*: A Practical Guide to Mission Audit. London: Scripture Union, 1991.

Foster, Roger. *Ten New Churches.* London: MARC Europe, 1986.

Galloway, Dale with Millis, Kathis. *The Small Group Book: The Practical Guide for Nurturing Christians and Building Churches.* Grand Rapids, Michigan, USA: Fleming H. Revell. A Division of Baker Book House Co., 1995.

George, Carl F. *Prepare Your Church for the Future*. Grand Rapids, Michigan, USA Fleming H. Revell. A Division of Baker Book House Co., 1992.

George, Carl F. with Warren Bird. *The Coming Church Revolution*: Empowering Leaders for the Future. Grand Rapids, Michigan, USA Fleming H. Revell. A Division of Baker Book House Co., 1994.

Gibbs, Eddie. *Ten Growing Churches*: London: MARC Europe, 1984.

Gladden, Ron. *Plant the Future: So Many Churches! Why Plant More?* USA: Pacific Press Publishing Association, 2000.

Greenaway, Roger S. *Guidelines For Urban Church Planting*. Grand Rapids, Michigan. USA: Baker Book House, 1976.

Hill, Mike. *Reaching The Unchurched*. UK: Scripture Press Foundation (UK) Ltd. Alpha. 1994.

Hull, Bill. *The Disciple-Making Church*. Grand Rapids, Michigan, USA: Fleming H. Revell. A Division of Baker Book House Co. 1990.

Hybels, Lynne & Bill. *Rediscovering Church*. Grand Rapid, Michigan, USA: Zondervan Publishing House, A Division of Harper Collins Publishers. 1995.

Hybels, Bill and Mittelberg, Mark. *Becoming a Contagious Christian*. Grand Rapids, Michigan, USA: Zondervan Publishing House, A Division of Harper Collins Publishers. 1994.

Johnson, Kim A. *Body Spiritual Building Manual*. Hagerstown, MD: Review and Herald, 1997.

Johnson, Kurt J. *Small Groups for the End-time*: A Practical Guide for the Twenty-first Century. Hagerstown, MD: Review and Herald Publishing Association, 1997.

Keirsey, David & Bates, Marilyn. *Please Understand Me*. California, USA: Prometheus Nemesis Book Company, Gnosology Books Ltd. 1984.

Kotter, John P. *Leading Change*. Boston, Massachusetts USA: Harvard Business School Press, 1996.

Kreider, Larry and Saunder, Brian. *Helping You Build Cell Churches*. PA. USA: DOVE Christian Fellowship International,1998.

Kroeger, Otto and Thuesen, Janet M. *Type Talk*. New York, USA: Dell Publishing Group, 1988.

Logan, Robert. *Beyond Church Growth*: Action Plans for Developing a Dynamic Church. Grand Rapids, Michigan, USA: Fleming H. Revell. A Division of Baker Book House, 1984.

Logan, Robert E. and Short, Larry. *Mobilising for Compassion: Moving People into Ministry*. Grand Rapids, Michigan, USA: Fleming H. Revell. A Division of Baker Book House, 1984.

Mayo, Bob. *Gospel Exploded*. Great Britain: Triangle, 1996.

Mead, Loren B. *The Once and Future Church: Reinventing the Congregation for a New Mission Frontier*. Washington DC, USA: The Alban Institute, Inc., 1994.

Neighbour, Ralph W. Jr. With Jenkins, Oorna. *Where Do We Go From Here*? A Guidebook for the Cell Church. Houston, Texas, USA: Touch Publications, Inc., 1990.

Oosterwal, Gottfried. *Mission Possible*. Nashville, Tennessee, USA: Southern Publishing Association, 1972.

Paulien, Jon. *Present Truth in the Real World*: The Adventist struggle to keep and share faith in a secular society. Ontario, Canada: Pacific Press Publishing Association, 1993.

Peck, M. Scott. *The Different Drum*: Community Making and Peace. USA: Touchstone, 1998.

——————— . *Further Along the Road Less Travelled*. USA: Touchstone, 1997.

——————— . *People of the Lie*: The Hope for Healing Human Evil. USA: Touchstone, 1998.

——————— . *The Road Less Travelled*. Great Britain: Hutchinson and Company. 1988.

Pippert, Rebecca Manley. *Out Of The Saltshaker*. Leicester: Inter-Varsity Press, 1979.

Richter, Philip and Francis, Leslie J. *Gone but not Forgotten. Church Leaving and Returning*. England: Darton, Longman and Todd Ltd. 1998.

Robinson, Martin. *A World Apart: Creating a Church for the Unchurced*. England: Monarch Publications, 1992.

Robinson, Martin with Christine, Stuart. *Planting Tomorrow's Churches Today*. Kent, England: Monarch Publications, 1988.

Samaan, Philip G. *Christ's Way of Making Disciples*. Hagerstown. USA: Review and Herald Publishing Association, 1999.

Schaller, Lyle E, *21 Bridges to the 21st Century*. Nashville, TN.: Abingdon Press, 1994.

Schwarz, Christian A. *Natural Church Development*. Spain: M.C.E. HOREB, Viladecavalls (Barcelona), 1996.

Shawchuck, Norman and Kotler Philip. *Marketing for Congregations: Choosing to Serve People More Effectively.* Nashville, TN, USA: Abingdon Press, 1992.

Singlehurst, Laurence. *Sowing, Reaping, Keeping.* Reading, Berkshire: Crossways Books, 1997.

Snyder, Howard A. *Radical Renewal: The Problem of Wineskins Today.* Houston, Texas, USA: Touch Publications.

Steinbron, Melvin J. *The Lay Driven Church.* California, USA: Regal Books. A Division of Gospel Light, 1997.

Stockstill, Larry. *The Cell Church. Preparing Your Church for the Coming Harvest* Ventura, California, USA: Regal, A Division of Gospel Light 1998.

Storey, Chris. *How to be Unbelievably Friendly.* England: Kingsway Publications, 1999.

Strobel. Lee. *Inside the Mind of Unchurched Harry & Mary.* Grand Rapids, Michigan, USA: Zondervan Publishing House, 1993.

Strommen, Merton P. *The Innovative Church.* USA: Augsburg Fortress, 1997.

Wagner, C. Peter. *Leading Your Church to Growth.* The Secret of Pastor/People Partnership in Dynamic Church Growth. Reading, Berks: Cox & Wyman Ltd, 1988.

Wagner, C. Peter. *Church Planting for a Greater Harvest.* California, USA: Regal Books. A Division of Gospel Light, 1990.

Wagner, C. Peter. *Strategies for Church Growth.* Europe: Kingsway Publications, Eastbourne for MARC. 1987.

Warren, Rick. *The Purpose Driven Church: Growth Without Compromising Your Message and Mission.* Grand Rapids, Michigan, USA: Zondervan Publishing House, 1995.

Webster, Douglas D. *Selling Jesus.* Illinois, USA: InterVarsity Press, 1992.

Yancey, Philip. *What's So Amazing About Grace?* Grand Rapids, Michigan, USA: Zondervan Publishing House. A Division of Harper Collins Publishers, 1997.

Index

How small groups help build, 129

.